FURTHER CONFESSIONS
OF A
SMALL PRESS RACKETEER

ALSO BY STUART ROSS

A Hamburger in a Gallery (DC Books, 2015)
In In My Dream (Bookthug, 2014)
A Pretty Good Year (NiB Publishing, 2014)
Nice Haircut, Fiddlehead (Puddles of Sky, 2014)
Our Days in Vaudeville (Mansfield Press, 2013)
You Exist. Details Follow. (Anvil Press, 2012)
Snowball, Dragonfly, Jew (ECW Press, 2011)
Cobourg Variations (Proper Tales Press, 2011)
I Have Come to Talk about Manners (Apt. 9 Press, 2010)
Buying Cigarettes for the Dog (Freehand Books, 2009)
Dead Cars in Managua (DC Books, 2008)
I Cut My Finger (Anvil Press, 2007)
Confessions of a Small Press Racketeer (Anvil Press, 2005)
Hey, Crumbling Balcony! Poems New & Selected (ECW Press, 2003)
Razovsky at Peace (ECW Press, 2001)
Home Shopping (Room 3O2 Books, 2000)
Farmer Gloomy's New Hybrid (ECW Press, 1999)
Henry Kafka & Other Stories (The Mercury Press, 1997)
The Inspiration Cha-Cha (ECW Press, 1996)
The Mud Game (w/ Gary Barwin, The Mercury Press, 1995)
Dusty Hats Vanish (Proper Tales Press, 1994)
The Pig Sleeps (w/ Mark Laba, Contra Mundo Books, 1993)
Runts (Proper Tales Press Press, 1992)
In This World (Silver Birch Press, 1992)
Mister Style, That's Me (Proper Tales Press, 1991)
Guided Missiles (Proper Tales Press, 1990)
Smothered (Contra Mundo Press, 1990)
Ladies & Gentlemen, Mr. Ron Padgett (Proper Tales Press, 1989)
Bunnybaby: The Child with Magnificent Ears (Proper Tales Press, 1988)
Paralysis Beach (Pink Dog Press, 1988)
Captain Earmuff 's Agenda (The Front Press, 1987)
Wooden Rooster (Proper Tales Press, 1986)
Skip & Biff Cling to the Radio (Proper Tales Press, 1984)
Father, the Cowboys Are Ready to Come Down from the Attic (Proper Tales Press, 1982)
When Electrical Sockets Walked Like Men (Proper Tales Press, 1981)
Bad Glamour (Proper Tales Press, 1980)
He Counted His Fingers, He Counted His Toes (Proper Tales Press, 1979)

TRANSLATION
My Planet of Kites, by Marie-Ève Comtois (trans. w/ Michelle Winters, Mansfield Press, 2015)

FURTHER CONFESSIONS
OF A
SMALL PRESS RACKETEER

Stuart Ross

ANVIL PRESS / VANCOUVER

Anvil Press Publishers Inc.
P.O. Box 3008, Main Post Office
Vancouver, B.C. V6B 3X5 CANADA
www.anvilpress.com

Library and Archives Canada Cataloguing in Publication

Ross, Stuart, author
        Further confessions of a small press racketeer / Stuart
Ross. — First edition.

Includes index.
ISBN 978-1-77214-018-7 (pbk.)

        1. Ross, Stuart. 2. Authors, Canadian (English)—20th
century—Biography. 3. Editors—Canada—Biography. 4. Small
presses—Canada. I. Title.

PS8585.O841Z464 2015   C818'.5409   C2015-901621-5

Printed and bound in Canada
Cover design by Rayola Graphic
Interior by HeimatHouse
Represented in Canada by the Publishers Group Canada
Distributed by Raincoast Books

The publisher gratefully acknowledges the financial assistance of the Canada Council for
the Arts, the Canada Book Fund, and the Province of British Columbia through the B.C.
Arts Council and the Book Publishing Tax Credit.

To the memory
of Lou Trifon, 1948–2014,
although I guess he'll never know

CONTENTS

INTRODUCTION

MOST OF THE essays in this book originally appeared, in earlier and sometimes more compact form, in the Vancouver-based lit mag *sub-Terrain*, where my column "Hunkamooga" had migrated when its first home, the Toronto-based *Word: A Literary Calendar*, shifted from physical object to online entity, a form I found less interesting. But a couple years ago, I had a falling-out with Brian Kaufman, *subTerrain*'s editor — and publisher of Anvil Press, with whom the volume you're holding right now is my fourth book — and killed my column. The time had come for "Hunkamooga" to die, anyway, at least for a while. I was struggling to come up with topics; things were feeling forced. Ever since I'd been served with papers from a lawyer in 2008, threatening me with a libel suit (for things I'd written on my blog, on social media, and by email, none of which, I maintain, were libellous), the kind of writing I did in "Hunkamooga" had become far more difficult. I was paranoid about future legal threats that might profoundly disrupt my life. That is the crippling effect of libel chill. It still boggles my mind and enrages me that my adversaries were themselves writers. Writers threatening other writers with libel suits. A week ago, a dozen people were murdered at the offices of Paris's satirical paper, *Charlie Hebdo*, not by writers, though, so far as we know. I guess I got off easy.

That fucking legal threat still torments me, obviously. Here it is, in the opening paragraph of this book, the sequel to 2005's *Confessions of a Small Press Racketeer*. I never apologized or retracted a thing I said; I just, finally, turned my back on it, and eventually it mostly went away. So, as the great Toronto mayor Rob Ford said a million times, the past is the past, it's time to move on.

Like I said, most of the material in this book comes from my "Hunkamooga" column, which I deep-sixed in 2012. The opening essay is a radically reworked version of something I wrote for an arts anthology published by Coach House Books. The interviews with Bruce Kauffman and Michael Dennis are pretty much verbatim from my blog, bloggamooga.blogspot.com. The memoir of Crad Kilodney is also from my blog. And there are a couple of other pieces here written specifically for this book, as well as a column about the Kootenays I started writing way back when, and then killed. I've resurrected it and completed it for this collection.

I write fiction, short and long, and I write poetry. I've published many books in those genres, but my book that has likely garnered the best response was *Confessions of a Small Press Racketeer*. Not sure why. A couple of years after we'd met, my partner Laurie and I discovered that she actually had one of my "Hunkamooga" columns pasted into her scrapbook. She'd put it there way before we'd first bumped into each other on Facebook. *Confessions* is still the book mentioned most often to me by other readers and writers I meet. I'd prefer that they mention my novel *Snowball, Dragonfly, Jew* or my story collection *Buying Cigarettes for the Dog* or my poetry book *Dead Cars in Managua*. But I'll take praise wherever the hell I can get it. I saw *Confessions* as a peripheral work, a set of footnotes, a "by the way," but I guess because it's so directly about my life, people connect most strongly with it.

The day after I killed "Hunkamooga," I put out the word that I was seeking a new home for it. I was surprised when there were no takers. Well, there was one offer, but without any money attached. I wanted to be paid to write these things. But in the end, it's just as well. Like I said, I was feeling a little bankrupt when it came to ideas. Since then, most of my essay energy has gone into a kind of memoir suggested to me by my friend Paul Vermeersch (one of my greatest defenders during Operation Libel Chill, resulting in us becoming close pals). I may or may not ever finish that book. I have a terrible memory ("Exploit the terribleness of your memory!" Paul encouraged me), and I've never kept a journal.

I try to tuck my own writing in wherever I can amid the freelance work I seem increasingly buried under. But some of that work is as important to me as my own writing. Right now, I'm editing a book of sonnets by David W. McFadden for Mansfield Press. It's the seventh book I've worked on with Dave. When I was a teenager, I idolized him. I hoped to someday meet him. I never imagined I'd become his friend and his editor. And I'm grateful to all the other literary presses and writers who make it impossible for me to dedicate enough time to my own writing by giving me proofreading and editing work. Somehow, amid it all, I do manage to squeeze my own books out.

As for me and Brian Kaufman, I'm still pissed off at him (it was a literary matter, but nothing related to my books with Anvil or my work with *subTerrain*). I wanted to do this second volume of essays, though, and he's the guy who has most supported me in the venture over the years. At first, I tried to put him off with outrageous contractual demands, but he agreed to all of them. The bastard.

So here I am. For me, it's all water under the bridges I've burned.

Stuart Ross
January 2015, Cobourg

IN THE SMALL-PRESS VILLAGE: NEW TRENDS IN ADEQUATE STAPLING

This essay originally appeared in the Coach House Books anthology The State of the Arts: Living with Culture in Toronto *in 2006. It has been substantially revised and updated for this book.*

TORONTO WAS ONCE home to nearly all of the country's major publishing companies, back at a time when Canada's big publishers were actually Canadian. Perhaps for that reason, the city also spawned many of the country's major small-press publishers — both the big small and the small small. And that's why I wound up standing in sub-zero temperatures with a handwritten sign around my neck reading "Writer Going to Hell: Buy My Books" and a couple of my self-published poetry chapbooks clenched in my frosty-gloved fist.

The major Toronto small presses born into the 1960s, including House of Anansi and Coach House, were essential to this country's revolution in fiction, and were the greatest champions — as small presses still are — of poetry. Coach House especially radicalized the physical concept of the book, as well, printing the things in strange shapes, in weird colours, and on a glorious array of paper stock. One of the trademarks of the small-press movement is the frequent marriage of a book's content and its form.

My focus here, though, is the small small press — publishing that occurs in someone's home or garage. People who, like me, have expended time, money, and friends doing this thing they love. People who fold and staple on their kitchen table, mass-photocopy at their workplace after hours, leave a trail of matchbook-size poetry magazines in telephone booths and on subway seats around the city. Joe O'Sullivan, who displayed his a scenario press output at the first Toronto Small Press Book Fair in 1987, sold poems he'd sealed into walnut shells. Poems on cheese sandwiches were also for sale nearby, and poems on the soles of old running shoes. There were mimeographed rants, tiny novels in pamphlet form, and — at Nicholas Power's Gesture Press table — comic strips about sentient potatoes.

My own small-press beginnings revolved around a 12-page chapbook I produced for a reading I gave at the Axletree Coffeehouse reading series in 1979. It was called *I Counted My Fingers, I Counted My Toes*, and — under the brand-new imprint Proper Tales Press — I made 50 unstapled copies. The next year I escalated to an edition of 1,000 copies of the poetry chapbook *Bad Glamour*, and I joined poet Don Garner and fictioneer Crad Kilodney on the streets of downtown Toronto, where we wore our dumb signs and sold books to thousands of passersby. At various times, we were joined by Michael Boyce, Mark Laba, and Lillian Necakov (all selling books by them I'd published through Proper Tales), and Arno Wolf Jr., a brilliant visual artist who wrote Gorey-like texts to accompany his Gorey-like drawings, and published through his Tantrum Press. My output, over three and a half decades, has included books both spineless and spiney, as well as leaflets, postcards, audio cassettes, CDs, zines, and broadsides.

The explosion of small presses and magazines in Toronto in the 1960s and '70s was unmatched anywhere in Canada, and even today no such phenomenon exists in Vancouver, Calgary, Montreal, or Halifax (though Ottawa is coming pretty close). Certainly there are lots of fine small presses across the country, but I'm talking concentration. Was it the proximity of the big presses that made Toronto a small-press nexus? A great deal of the credit probably also goes to the late, great writer and small presser bpNichol, beloved bpNichol, who, even as he was writing TV scripts for *Fraggle Rock*, sitting on the editorial collective of Coach House Press, winning awards, and publishing volume after volume of his sprawling life work, *The Martyrology*, continued his grOnk project: publishing mimeographed and photocopied poetry leaflets and booklets. bp, who died far too early at 44 in 1988, was a great role model, and a fountain of encouragement and generosity. A quieter but equally important presence in Toronto was Nelson Ball, whose impeccably mimeographed Weed/Flower books published early volumes by many greats (Davids McFadden, UU, and Rosenberg, George Bowering, bill bissett, Victor Coleman) and inspired other small publishers. Following in the footsteps of these two small-press legends was jwcurry, whose Curvd H&z is probably the most inventive, prolific press Canada has ever seen.

jw's in Ottawa now, doing naked readings, conducting sound-poetry symphonies, and constructing impossible books; Nelson is in Paris, Ontario, where he spent a couple decades with his now-late partner, the artist, writer, and sometime bp collaborator Barbara Caruso, writing his tiny perfect poems about sparrows, hyphens, and spring; and bp is — unbelievably — nearly three decades gone, but still read, revered, and emulated.

So what's left in Toronto? An eclectic community of poetry publishers, self-publishers, lit-mag makers, comic artists, and zine creators. It's not all that different from a few decades ago, but it's also, well, very different. Some would argue there is no such thing as a "small-press community" in Toronto. Instead, the creators of small-press literature and objects are wildly varying clusters of poets, zine makers, self-published novelists, book artisans, photocopy addicts, online zinesters, and comic book creators.

But this *is* the community. There are people in Toronto I admire, people who intrigue me, people who piss me off, and many I don't even talk with anymore (though perhaps there are more who would prefer not to talk with *me*). There is support, conspiracy, copulation, collaboration, libel, libel chill, and back stabbing. Just like there has always been. When one spoken-word poet died young and impoverished, others rallied to raise money to buy the poor sucker a headstone. When a self-proclaimed experimental poet went off his rocker and began spewing ad hominem bile in the name of "good writing," he got voted off the island by the lynch-mob masses while a couple of others futilely tried to reach out to him. When a small-presser and esoteric bookseller was behind in his rent and impoverished, a hundred or so literary types gathered at a pub and raised money for him. And when a legendary literary press was in danger of losing its home — and thus its existence — to a greedy landlord, thousands of writers and readers from Toronto and far beyond signed a petition and wrote letters of support.

Some people know they're participating in a community: in fact, sometimes that's the reason they publish. But others aren't aware that they are part of a community: they staple and fold in tight-jawed solitude, certain their poems about the World's Problems are going to change that world, unaware that anyone has ever done this before. *This* is community.

The exciting aspects of community rise above the pain it inevitably brews. The exchange of ideas, support, publications. Someone steps forward to start a reading series simply to benefit the art, to provide a forum for the kind of writing she likes. A couple of writers with entirely different aesthetics get together to collaborate on a poem, or a sequence, or a novel. A couple of small-pressers, frustrated by the problem of distribution, unite to create a monthly booksale for the micro and the ephemeral.

When I sold books on the street, my immediate community was Crad Kilodney and Don Garner, who had preceded me out there with signs around their own necks. There were also my high school creative-writing-class friends: Mark, Anne, Ashraf, Steven, Liane, and Mako. And the gang from George Miller's Axletree Coffeehouse workshop, some of whom published tiny editions and some of whom are still writing 40 years later. Oh, and John Robert Colombo, Canada's premiere propagator of found poetry, who borrowed books from the library near Bathurst and Lawrence where I was a teenage page. I didn't look for any of these people; I found them, they found me, we found ourselves in the same room. Of my high school pals, only Mark Laba went on to become a small-presser: the CEO of Psycho Potato Press, a rubber-stamped empire of demento-surrealism.

At my old high school, for several years, I led creative-writing work-shops that ended with each student publishing her poetry in an edition large enough to trade with each of the other students, plus a copy for me. There were books in beer bottles, books on toilet-paper rolls, books in the form of paper hats. In a day, a dozen small presses would be born. I was in ecstasy. And the kids were pretty happy too. Little did they know, they were the newest recruits in the small-press community.

But has the steam dissipated in the Toronto small-press movement in the last couple of decades? Has a generation more brainwashed by commerce and saddled with insane Toronto rents decided it's nuts to lose money on literature? There was a time when one looked eagerly for new chapbooks published by Kevin Connolly's Pink Dog Editions, Gil Adamson's Two Bints Press, Maggie Helwig's Lowlife Publishing, Crad Kilodney's Charnel House, Lillian Necakov's Surrealist Poets' Gardening Assoc., Jim Smith's The Front Press, and Daniel Jones's Streetcar Editions. Crad and Daniel are gone, and none of the rest are publishing chapbooks anymore (though Jim occasionally threatens to).

For a while there, it seemed like the chapbook generation was history. One of the only new torchbearers was Jay MillAr, whose BookThug spans the chapbook and the vertebrate, the unknown writer and the established. BookThug started off as a very personal project, under the name Boondoggle Books, before it became the major small press it is today. There was also Carleton Wilson, designer and typesetter extraordinaire, doing great things with his Junction Books, which is now an imprint of the B.C.-based Nightwood Editions.

Why, as the means of production became increasingly accessible, did the output diminish? Once upon a time I worked a typesetting machine that was the size of a kicked-over phone booth. The copy it spooled out had to go through trays of photographic developer and stabilizer. I hung to dry the unfurled scrolls of copy, before I could fasten them onto boards with melted wax, stripping in corrections with an X-acto knife. It's a lot easier now that people have computers. Typesetting machines have long been homes for radioactive rats in city dumps.

Did the internet railroad the small-press community? There was a long stretch when more Toronto writers seemed to have blogs than presses, leaning toward self-promotion and public-diary-making as opposed to cranking out physical editions of their own poetry or fiction, or work by their friends and those they admired. As a species, we seemed to spend more time surfing and blogging than folding and stapling. And while there are some interesting online mags, for those of us whose fetish is the physical book, it's a cumbersome practice reading good writing on a screen, and our fingertips miss the pleasing tactile experience.

And, just as it's always been, there are few commercial outlets for the products of literary small presses. The increasingly few indie bookstores and mini-chains carry a few titles, but the big-box stores and Amazonmonsters have killed many of them off; MillAr's Apollinaire's Books has an online presence and Jay himself used to show up with book displays at readings. Tara Azzopardi and Michael Comeau briefly sold small press through their short-lived Utopian gallery shop, Penny Arcade, in Kensington Market some years back. One of the powers behind the small press Quattro Books recently had a similarly short-lived small-press bookstore on College Street. But there's still no one place you can go, any day of the year, to pick up the new Gary Barwin, Jessica Bebenek, Dani Couture, or Andrew Faulkner. Except the collectively run Spineless Books on Harbord Street, and that exists only in my head.

Now, the Toronto Small Press Book Fair is finally dead; in its last years there was more excitement about it on the part of publishers than readers. It was a soupy, undiscerning, under-promoted monster by the time it croaked, struggling to draw a crowd twice a year. In the fair's golden age, small-pressers arranged their publishing schedules around it: in other words, the night before the event, they were furiously photocopying, folding, stapling, sewing, collating.

The Toronto Small Press Book Fair started up as a once-a-year event in 1987. It was the more ambitious child of Meet the Presses, a monthly reading/booksale for small presses that Nicholas Power and I ran at the Scadding Court Community Centre throughout 1985. With funding from the Canada Council's National Book Week, we held the bigger fair at Innis College Pub, where about 40 small presses put on their best for about 500 members of the public. We also published the first *Instant Anthology* that day: writers showed up in the morning with a page of poetry or prose; a team of editors made their choices at lunchtime; and some frantic volunteers ran the book through an on-site photocopier (and the photocopier down the lane at Coach House, who saved us when ours broke down) and collated the thing for sale at the end of the day.

The next year, the fair moved to the Trinity-St. Paul Centre in the Annex, and Kevin Connolly filled Nick's shoes. We squeezed in about 60 presses and mags, and about 1,000 civilians. I'd do one more fair after that (with Nick again), and then we'd pass the mantle to the first of a series of new coordinators. (Before the fair's decline, it was run by the likes of Clint Burnham, Daniel Jones, Victor Coleman, Alice Burdick, Katy Chan, Maggie Helwig, Maria Erskine, Beth Follett, Nicky Drumbolis, and Kristiana Clemens.)

For me, the fair at its best was the community in action. It crossed genres, cliques, classes, and colours. Early birds helped set up the chairs and tables, and laggards helped close the shindig down. Sister Vision would end up sitting beside *Mr. Magnanimous*, ECW beside *Eat Me, Literally*. It was the greatest gathering place/time for the anarchic guerrilla units that make up the small-press community. Some publishers spent much of their day scurrying from table to table, seeing what was out there while abandoning their own displays; others sat cross-armed behind their tables for seven hours straight, absolutely uninterested in what anyone else was publishing or else reluctant to leave their table lest they miss a single sale. It was the focus of the Toronto small press: all the young publishers were there, plus the usual grumpy vets like John Laughlin of Sherwood Press and Paul Dutton of Underwhich.

Somewhere along the line, the Toronto Small Press Fair started happening twice a year, and its zest began to flag. In 2008, I blogged critically about the fair's organization; the organizers sent a lawyer after me; it got mighty fucking ugly; and there was a terrible rupture in the city's small-press scene. What had happened to the once-vibrant fair? Had familiarity and predictability lessened interest in it? There seemed to be more people selling jewellery and crafts. The event had sprawled beyond its original literary intent. And the room was no longer as easily filled. Those first few hours, especially, when publishers outnumbered the public, were harrowing.

Things had really changed since the first Toronto Small Press Book Fair in 1987. What we once considered small presses didn't seem so small anymore. With the exception of the poetry they continued to champion, Coach House, ECW, and Mercury were producing books that seemed increasingly like the fare put out by the mainstream presses, and the physical form of the book often emulated that model too. Most of these presses no longer bothered with tables at the Small Press Book Fair, maybe because they didn't sell much there, maybe because they felt too old among all the teen zine-makers and poetry broadsiders. Still, these presses were the mentors for much smaller presses, and occasionally the pricks against which the small small presses kicked.

In 1989, Nick Power wrote in the Small Press Book Fair catalogue, "Why would anyone want to do small press? The rewards are not obvious to the commercially minded: rarely is there a profit margin, expense accounts, or, in fact, any salary. There aren't the usual book trade benefits either — the glitzy launch parties and book tours. Most small press publishers are ignored by the conventional reviewing media. So, what is it that motivates the small press beast?"

Into the 1990s, Nick's questions went beyond the rhetorical. There seemed to be a new emphasis on blatant self-promotion and what some (including me) have disparagingly called "careerism"; cranking out little stapled chapbooks wasn't consistent with this art-capitalism. Young writers seemed too often to leap directly to books with big small presses, avoiding the chapbook phase in their careers. While such presses often allowed their writers greater involvement in the production of the book than a mainstream press would tolerate, these writers were missing out on the visceral experience of conceiving of and constructing the physi-

21

cal package for their writing, of handing their books directly to potential readers and of becoming part of a glorious community of misfits.

It might be that the presses and the chapbooks were no longer the heart of the community: the readings were. For a generation of "careerist" writers, readings were better promotional tools than lowly chapbooks, and they offered more immediate ego-fulfillment. Toronto, with its broad spectrum of literary events — sometimes there are as many as eight or ten readings and launches on a single night! — was still a bubbling laboratory of new and adventurous writing. It just wasn't being manifested in the way it once was. Had personality and live performance become more important than the work itself? Did anybody revel anymore in the physical feel of the book, its smell, its heft or its beautiful ephemerality? I worried — along with many of my colleagues who grew into this scene in the 1970s and 1980s — that I was becoming a dinosaur.

Young writers were jockeying for position as a "feature" at the Art Bar, Pivot, Livewords, Rowers, and tons more. And, crumpled spoken-word texts stuffed into their gumball-sticky pockets, mostly predictable rhymers increasingly made the rounds of the open mics, shouting, berating, and rapping. Spoken word is far more about personality — and marketing — than about text, while small press depends on the printed page. The community had simply found new places to congregate: bars where readings happen, where they'd often sooner spend a fin on a pint than a chapbook.

The readings are still going strong; a new series or two probably got started after I began writing the last paragraph. Jess Taylor has started up the popular Emerging Writers Reading Series at the divey Duffy's Tavern on Bloor West; Hoa Nguyen and Dale Smith operate the Skanky Possum series out of their east-end living room, while Jay and Hazel MillAr host the HIJ series out of their west-end living room. Skanky offers up vegan grub along with the words, while HIJ bakes pies. Bänoo Zan runs the monthly Shab-e She'r at Beit Zatoun, and the weekly Sunday Poetry Presents fills up Ellington's Café.

But physical publications have been making a comeback. Out of the chaos of the mudslinging and threats of 2008's libel chill attack on me, a new collective emerged: Meet the Presses, taking the name of the 1985 series Nick and I had created. Co-founders included Nick and I, along with several other former organizers of the once-great Toronto Small Press Book Fair — Beth, Maggie, Maria — and some other active, dedicated small-pressers. We started off slowly, and eventually created the Indie Literary Market: a smaller, more focused, curated small-press sale.

At the same time, exciting new presses sprouted: The Emergency Response Unit, Toronto Poetry Vendors, Grow + Grow, Odourless Press, Horses of Operation, and more. Meet the Presses has put on several very successful curated literary markets — one devoted entirely to chapbooks — as well as a small-press variety show and a workshop conducted by American poet Gabriel Gudding. Coach House Books, revitalized over the past decade by head editor Alana Wilcox, participates at the markets, as do the tiniest of micropresses. And Meet the Presses has taken over administration of the annual bpNichol Chapbook Award, stirring up even more interest in folding and stapling, especially since the award purse rocketed to $4,000 in 2014, thanks to the prize's anonymous benefactor, who has more than filled the financial void since the award left the hands of its previous administrators, the Phoenix Foundation.

At the fall 2014 market, where small-pressers from Toronto, Hamilton, Buffalo, Ottawa, Kingston, London, and Cobourg (that's me!) congregated, there was a sense of community in the room rivalling that of the 1980s. Yes, there are some very fine online mags and chapbook presses these days, but there seems to be renewed excitement about the physical book. There were as many young people as there were geezers like me. And small-press curmudgeons Paul Dutton and John Laughlin were still at it, standing behind their books. Well, sitting behind their books, anyway.

The community lives. The Small Press Beast is on the prowl.

JUST ANOTHER MENTOR CASE

TWO FLOORS ABOVE This Ain't the Rosedale Library, there were wails of grief and self-pity. How come Toronto isn't like New York? How come our poets must wander the streets in a mentorless daze?

I brought Hoboken, New Jersey, poet Joel Lewis to Toronto last month to read at my Kat Biscuits! series, and Jay MillAr offered him a spot at the Speakeasy, an event where poets talk about their work. First Sandra Alland spoke about her Beckett-translation project, and then Joel took the floor, reading from a memoir of his five-year acquaintanceship with New York's Ted Berrigan, who died in 1983. It was neat, because Sandra worked bpNichol into her talk, and I've always seen strong parallels (including dedication to literary experimentation, autobiographical poeming, collaboration, soft-drink consumption) between bp and Berrigan.

Anyway, Joel was absorbing, funny, and occasionally moving. The focus of his manuscript, he explained, was mentorship. Ted had been his mentor. The small Toronto audience was enchanted, taken by Joel's exoticness (his strong Brooklyn accent, the occasional Yiddish word, and his coffee-bean tie), and during the Q&A there were cries that we have no such mentors here. The ululations erupted from a spot somewhere between outrage and resignation. Talk on the listservs the next day touched on how different the literary scenes are in the U.S. and Canada.

But I don't buy it. It's an issue of era, not geography. Joel was talking about the late 1970s — around the same time, bpNichol, a decade Berrigan's junior, played a similar role among young poets here. Both these guys were, to some degree, products of the hippie era, embracing a communal philosophy, a world of open doors. And housing was cheaper and grants more dependable in the '70s. One could afford a lot more time for others and for one's writing.

I started thinking about my own mentors. When I was in my mid-teens and a page at Bathurst Heights Library, the writer John Robert Colombo, known best for his found poetry, came in each week. We had a lot of his books on our shelves there: *The Mackenzie Poems*, *The Great Wall of China*, *Neo Poems*, *Abracadabra*, and *John Toronto*. He was a charismatic man, with a touch of flamboyance and a healthy ego. He lived just a few blocks from the library. I introduced myself to him and told him I wrote poetry. He said something like "Well, you know what young poets do — they apprentice established poets!" And soon I found myself apprenticing John Robert Colombo for a couple of years. I worked as a sort of gofer for him — I proofread the bluelines of his books, snipped quotations from his big book of Canadian quotations and arranged them by topic for his concise book of Canadian quotations, and — my most exotic assignment — laden with plastic bags filled with all of science-fiction writer and anthologist Judith Merril's anthologies, I trundled down to Judy's *Ideas* office at CBC headquarters on Jarvis Street, where she set me up at a photocopier and I photocopied all the little italicized introductions Judy had written to pre-cede each story in all the anthologies. In exchange, John imparted his wisdom about poetry, and critiqued my poems, which were typewritten (manual) on sheets of yellow foolscap. God, I wrote bad poems then. He wrote some pretty bad poems too.

At Bathurst Heights Library I also met library clerk Michael Richardson, about 15 years my senior and British. Somehow his accent gave everything he said a great deal of weight. Michael knew everything about the contemporary and the avant-garde. From him I learned about artists Jim Dine and Larry Rivers, writers B. S. Johnson and Jeff Nuttall, musicians Robert Wyatt and Ivor Cutler, gay raconteur Quentin Crisp, and lots more. Michael also did some work for John Colombo, and wound up editing a couple of intriguing fiction anthologies. Jeannie Richardson, Michael's then-wife, was — and is — an amazing painter. As a teenage writer, I was pretty thrilled to have this hip arts couple as friends.

In high school, I studied creative writing with a series of guys who nurtured and encouraged young writers: David Young and Victor Coleman from Coach House Press, Joe Rosenblatt, and Sam f. Johnson. Young and Coleman were crazy writers then, tapped into all the crazy writing that was happening — books like *The Strange Odyssey of Howard Pow and Other Stories* by nutcase Bill Hutton. Writers like Fielding Dawson, Ed Dorn, Jack Spicer, and Michael Ondaatje. That was in the days of *The Collected Works of Billy the Kid* and *Rat Jelly* — Ondaatje was freaky then. Both Young and Coleman had us write in all sorts of crazy ways: we *experimented*! Victor sometimes wrote under the name Vic D'Or in those days, and at the hippie house where he lived, his room had a sign taped onto the entrance: *Vic's D'Or*.

Rosenblatt, with whom we spent a week at our school and at the "coffee room" of Coach House Press, was a real character, and a huge influence on my childhood friend (and one of Canada's greatest nearly unknown poets) Mark Laba. He spoke in a low rumble-mumble, but was a brilliant sound poet whose *Bumblebee Dithyramb* was the most exciting poetry book I'd ever seen. At some point, he had us all come to his house

27

to address envelopes for the mailing of the mag he edited, *Jewish Dialogue*. He fed us Ritz crackers and beer. Johnson, who visited our school weekly for a while, was comparatively normal: he was a gentle soul with a blond-red Robin Hood beard, and was part of a loose movement in Toronto in those days called the House Poets, which included wacky Alfred Rushton and burly poet cop Hans Jewinski.

Somehow — I think it was after a conference for high school writers — Mark and I ended up downtown at Harbourfront on weekends, part of a poetry workshop led by a tall, thoughtful, generous guy named George Miller and built around the Axletree Coffeehouse reading series, held then at the old Trinity Church, behind the Eaton's Centre. George's voice sounds like it's coming from the profound depths of the ocean. His laugh charms and warms you. He was practically a cult leader to us.

The era I'm talking about is 1974 to 1979 or so. Around the time that Ted Berrigan was urging the straight-laced Joel Lewis to become a speed freak, or at least an alcoholic. If a mentor is defined as an elder poet who encourages you, I had a whole bunch of them back in that period.

Soon after that, Tom Walmsley, a writer connected with Pulp Press, wrote the introduction to my novel *Father, the Cowboys Are Ready to Come Down from the Attic.* And D. M. Fraser, a short-story writer now long gone and sadly neglected, had scrawled all over that manuscript, showing me how the thing should be done. They scared me, these hard-drinking Vancouver writers, but they prodded me on and gave me their time.

That was then, and this is now. I still have mentors of sorts. David McFadden is a mentor by example. I mean, he's a friend too, but willing to impart his incredible knowledge, though it might take a couple glasses of wine. And Paul Dutton, over the years, has often shared his sound-poetry wisdom with me. Paul's a tough customer, but he challenges me in a good way.

I have other mentors, too, who aren't part of the literary world. They're people who influenced the very way I think: Robin Wood, the film critic and teacher from Atkinson College at York University; Carl Funk (now Carl Harrison), my high school history teacher, and my friend nearly 30 years later.

More recently, I was in New York in January for a "master class" workshop with Ron Padgett. The poet and teacher Larry Fagin invited me to drop by his apartment. The two hours I spent there, listening to his stories, looking at the art on his walls, taking a tour through the books and magazines he's published, sharing a bit of Toronto with him — these were two profoundly important hours for me. And my post-workshop subway rides with Padgett, where the talk was small and warm, are something I'll cherish too. Are these remarkable guys mentors? I may never see them again. I met them; they gave of their time; I learned.

As you get older, the lines sometimes begin to blur. Mentors become friends, and friends become colleagues, and the playing field is gradually levelled. But if I'd been Ted Berrigan, I would've told Joel Lewis to lose the coffee-bean tie. I mean, really.

March 2005

I did see Ron Padgett again, and Larry Fagin, many times. I studied with Larry for a while, too. And I published a book by Ron Padgett — If I Were You, a collection of collaborations. Still in touch with Joel Lewis, as well, and see him occasionally on my trips to New York. He's a very fine poet, and you can see streaks of his mentor, Ted Berrigan, running through his work.

As for John Robert Colombo, my first mentor, he and I wound up appearing at the same literary festival in Collingwood just a few years ago. I saw on the schedule that he was doing a reading at a small local art gallery, so I decided to go. He was still the same charmer. He told the audience he was the only poet in the world who published one book a year made up of all the poems he wrote that year. He read a selection of his poems and aphorisms, and it was thoroughly entertaining. I approached him afterwards and told him who I was. He was surprised and mentioned that I'd put on weight. We hadn't seen each other for about 25 years. I had, indeed, put on weight.

FUNNY, YOU DON'T LOOK
KOOTENAY

ALBERTA POET AND performance artist Ali Riley and I are walking along the main street of New Denver, B.C., population 600. From behind us, a woman calls our names, then catches up to us.

Turns out she's from *The Valley Voice*, and she'd like us to offer up some quotes about the students at Lucerne School, where we've been conducting poetry workshops this week. In the *Voice* office, a guy slides us a steno pad and says, "We don't have much space — could we just get a short quote."

I'm stymied. It all seems so general. "Aren't you supposed to ask me some questions and get what you want out of me?" I ask.

"You know," he replies, "just something about how great they are to work with."

Turns out his son is among the students in my classes. Ali and I comply, managing to come up with interesting ways to express the thrill of teaching here in this tiny town surrounded by the mountains.

A couple of blocks away, I pop into Sappho's Bakery for some bread and a few oatmeal cookies. Turns out I'm also teaching the son of the woman who's serving me there. Also, I'm amazed that a town of 600 can have a Sappho's Bakery. Such are the mysteries of the Kootenays.

I'm staying for a couple of weeks in a small, beautiful cabin on Slocan Lake. A big-city boy, I'd never lit a wood stove before, but now I'm a pro. Out back there's a three-seater outhouse, from the property's past life as a kids' school. From my headquarters in the woods, I make forays into New Denver, nearby Nakusp, and distant Kimberley and Cranbrook, putting small-town kids through my crazy poetry strategies, and reading my poems in community halls, cafés, and bookstores.

There are some really fine young writers out here, and some teens who are simply struggling to find a way to express themselves. Aside from my school visits, I do a couple of two-day, off-site residencies for the New Denver and Nakusp kids who are most interested in writing. And while they're going through their odd experience of spending time with a surrealist poet from Toronto, I'm going through my own transformation.

First, I'm proud I can use an outhouse and a wood stove. I also kayak for my first time and explore the woods and beaches with Tess, a magnificent dog I get to borrow for my hikes. When I wake each morning, I lift my head a few inches and peer through some trees, across a lake, at mountains and glaciers. Everything is calm here, the air is pure, there are no sounds of traffic.

Terry Taylor, the Lucerne School writing and English teacher, conspired with Jeff Pew, the Selkirk Secondary School writing teacher in Kimberley, about five hours away across the terrifying Salmo-Creston Pass, to bring me here after I worked briefly with their kids in Banff during WordFest 2003. They are extraordinary people, and their writing students are smart, enthusiastic, and challenging. Terry and Jeff also drew in a vice-principal and writer of stage musicals at nearby Nakusp Secondary School. All three organize small but ambitious writing festivals in their respective towns.

I wonder what happens when a town like New Denver has no Terry Taylor. I guess there's no writers' festival, perhaps no writing course at the high school. Once upon a time she had wanted to be a bigger fish, a journalist, but she thought she'd teach for a year — and she's still at it a couple decades later. I can't imagine a bigger or more important fish. How astonishing to be in a place where you can actually make a difference. The nine young writers who attend my residency here might not be writers if it weren't for Terry.

Jeff Pew does the same damn thing in Kimberley, where he organizes the Poetry on the Rocks festival. This year he's brought in me and Leslie Greentree, who wrote *Go-go Dancing for Elvis*, and a couple of intense hippie performance poets from Seattle named Steve and Tammy. We do a heap of workshops in the local high school and then read to an overcapacity crowd at the Bean Tree Café in the Platzl, their weird little faux-Bavarian downtown. I crash at Jeff's place on my last night in Kimberley, and he and I collaborate on a poem and watch a DVD of bill bissett and bpNichol being interviewed by Phyllis Webb, circa 1968. I feel like I've known Jeff for years, instead of just days.

After two life-changing weeks in the Kootenays, including a near-death experience on the Salmo-Creston Pass (i.e., I drove over it, at about 40 km per hour, Neil Diamond coming out the speakers), I make the cruel nine-hour drive back to Vancouver, arriving at Clint Burnham's place just an hour before my book launch at the artist-run centre Artspeak. The new book is *Confessions of a Small Press Racketeer*, from Anvil Press, and the printer promised to deliver books that morning to the publisher's apartment. I was skeptical, and a nervous wreck, but there it was. There's a lot more going on in Vancouver on a Saturday night than in New Denver, and attendance at the launch is a bit thin.

But that's okay, because, as Nick Power points out to me a week later at the Toronto Small Press Book Fair, I've made a terrible mistake in my book, my horrible book: I wrote that the first fair — which Nick and I organized — took place at Hart House. It actually took place at the Innis College Pub, and that's why I write these words from the solitary confinement wing of the Toronto Small Press Penitentiary. In the morning, they're shaving my head. Ah, the three-seater outhouse of New Denver seems so far away…

May 2005 (but not previously published)

The Kootenays, since 2005, has taken on a huge role in my life. I've returned there to teach nearly every year since. The Kootenays have also expanded my understanding of Canada, what Canada is. And that little cabin in the woods by the lake is my second home now. Terry Taylor has moved from teaching into administration, but is always cooking up exciting new literary adventures for students in the region — festivals, workshops, distance learning, and more. Jeff Pew and I have written many more collaborative poems, and the son of the excellent and dedicated Valley Voice *folks — Owain Peach Nicholson — is becoming a Canadian poet to contend with. If one believes in contending.*

I HATE POETRY!

I'M ABOUT TO dive into my novel for a month or two, so I thought I'd get in one more kick at the poetry can. It's a good time for that, because I've spent most of the past weekend at my first-ever League of Canadian Poets annual general meeting.

I avoided joining the League for many years, and perhaps part of the reason was its dorky name. It made me feel like I needed to don a red cape or something, maybe some goggles and silver boots. But there's also a feeling out there among many of my colleagues that the organization is a bit flaky and might be filled with the Sunday scratchers of many poems of the grandmother and cat genres.

I haven't been a League member long enough to know if any of that is true. The AGM weekend suggested that the organization represents the full gamut, but with a notable shortage on the experimental end of the spectrum.

But here's the sauce: people were talking about poetry as if it's this inherently good thing that should be promoted. There were comments like "It's important to give poetry a higher profile among the public." And the League's interim executive director, after delivering her upbeat report to the gathered membership, said that she enjoyed her job — one of the reasons being, "I love poetry."

I've heard that before, and I don't think it can really be. I mean, if you said, "I love music," that would mean you love Whitesnake, Patsy Cline, William Walton, CCMC, and Ashlee Simpson. Oh, also the Chipmunks. Although each represents the pinnacle of musical genius, no one loves *all* of them.

So when someone says, "I love poetry," and I've heard it pretty often, does it mean they love Christian Bök, Salvatore Quasimodo, Rod McKuen, Roo Borson, Chaucer, David UU, James Tate, Ogden Nash, d.a. levy, Margaret Christakos, Carmine Starnino (god forbid!), Richard Thomas, Alexander Pope, and Suzanne Somers? Not to mention every goddamn poem about loneliness by every zit-squeezing teenager who ever lived. Plus this poem I wrote when I was 11: "When you double a bubble, / you have two bubbles, but this information isn't worth / a pile of rubble." (The *Toronto Star* rejected it, the bastards!)

I chatted with Paul Dutton about it this afternoon and he says that people who say they love poetry are enamoured with the *idea* of poetry, rather than with actual poems. I'm enamoured with the idea of *good* poems. But how much of what gets published do I actually like? Ten per cent? Five per cent? Probably it's more like one per cent. So that means I dislike 99 per cent of poetry, and it would be more fitting for me to say, "I hate poetry." I'd probably make more friends that way, too.

To put a more positive spin on it, though, I would say that I like poetry that I like. In fact, I like 100% of the poetry that I like. I'm happy to promote my own poetry, and promote the poetry I enjoy, but I can't get whipped up by the League's blanket determination to give poetry a wider public profile. In fact, I think a lot of my League brothers and sisters would be better off putting their energy into writing good poems and reading Bill Knott until their eyes bleed.

Anyway, just last night I promoted some poetry that needed promoting. I took part in an event in the Art Bar Poetry Series called Canadian

Poetry Night. The idea was that each of the invited writers would read the works of another Canadian writer. I chose to read a couple of poems by David UU, a sound/visual/text poet who no one ever talks about anymore and who I suspect most younger poets have never heard of. David killed himself in 1994, and left behind an uneven but fascinating body of work.

After I picked the poems I wanted to read, I wrestled with how to read them. I decided to go with a low-key near-drone because I didn't want to inflict my own persona on David's stuff. I was last up, with 15 poets reading before me, and I was afraid I'd be a bit of a downer. But the response David's work got was amazing. One young woman there said that David's poetry made the evening worthwhile for her — that she was moved nearly to tears. I even received a few emails today by people who'd never heard of him and were intrigued.

I think my dragging out those UU poems made some writers aware that there's a history out there that they're not familiar with. Poets struggle during their lifetime and often take their careers with them when they die. I'd love to see a League of Canadian Poets AGM where we don't promote poetry, per se — we celebrate the works of worthy poets who have died. Because we're all going to be dead someday, guaranteed, and while it's nice that our physical books will outlive us, it'd be nice to know that someone out there in the land of the living is reading our work and sharing it.

June 2005

Not sure if the League took my last-paragraph advice. I never got to another AGM — in fact, I don't think I ever renewed my membership.

37

THE LOST SUBWAY RIDE

I AM LYING in bed in the basement guestroom of my dear cousin Fern's glorious cabin in Stony Plain, southwest of Edmonton. At the foot of the bed is a small bookshelf, mainly filled with children's books. I take out Roald Dahl's *The Twits* and open it to the title page. There is a child's signature carefully recorded in pencil there: *Leanne.*

I'm holding in my hands a book that Leanne held in her hands, a book in which she wrote her name. I sit back in bed and read *The Twits*, my first Roald Dahl ever. Leanne, I discover, had good taste.

Leanne Palylyk was killed by a drunk driver on June 25, 1988, when she was a measly 11 years old. She was travelling with her friend and her friends' parents. After the crash, her friend was an orphan with one fewer friend.

Leanne wanted to be a writer. In fact, she already was one. When Fern, along with Leanne's grandmother Toby, decided to fulfill one of Leanne's great dreams and publish a book of her writings, they took me on as editor and sent me a huge envelope of my little cousin's stories and poems. There were rhyming poems and non-rhymers, poems written on some whimsy, and some for special holidays or for her grandmother. There were also lots of stories, some unfinished. One of those stories was "Greenoli" — it was about 20 pages long and there were two very different drafts in the envelope.

An 11-year-old doing a radically revised draft of a short story? Leanne would have been about 27 years old now, and she'd probably have stories published in *Malahat Review*, in *Fiddlehead*, in *Grain*, who knows where. I'd have pestered her into self-publishing a chapbook. Or perhaps she'd have a book out already from Thistledown or Random House.

Instead she has a single posthumous book out (I can't believe I'm typing "posthumous" about an 11-year-old). It's called *The Flashback Storm*, and we did 1,000 copies of it to raise money for People Against Impaired Drivers, an organization Fern became passionately involved in after Leanne's death. *The Flashback Storm* contains "Greenoli," plus several other tales, and a dozen or so of Leanne's playful poems. Much of this is ambitious stuff — mature and adventurous.

I found something else among the papers Fern sent me. It was a letter Leanne had written to me but never sent. I was the only writer she knew, and she wondered if she had the right stuff. I guess she was planning on mailing me this letter along with a few of her pieces. I know what it's like to write a letter and never get around to sending it. But I'm glad I finally received it. A few years have passed now, but I think I closed my teary eyes and answered her letter in my head, hoping she'd hear it.

A while before she died, the family met in Hamilton for our cousin Daniel's bar mitzvah. God, everyone was alive then: my mother and father, and my brother Owen (though I don't think he came to Hamilton that day). Leanne was there, wearing a cast (on her leg? her arm? I don't remember). There was a lovely celebration in Daniel's family's backyard, and I was sitting on a bench with Leanne and her little brother Tony. Their sister Nirah was running around in the huge backyard nearby. We were having a blast, playing and chattering away and goofing around. I thought, "Hey, kids like me!" These were the first kids I had ever had a rapport with, as an adult. I'd always felt awkward around kids before. But

Leanne and Tony seemed to genuinely enjoy my company, and so did Nirah, and I certainly enjoyed theirs. We made plans for an adventure: in a few days, I'd take Leanne and Tony downtown on the Toronto subway. It was a big deal, and I was giddy about this new experience. But for whatever reason, that journey never transpired, and a year or so later, when my mother told me Leanne had been killed, I immediately thought of that lost subway ride. I wanted so much to go back in time and do whatever I had to do to make it happen.

My mother was devastated by Leanne's death. Our cousins' children were the grandchildren my parents never had. (I mean, really, what the hell was going on with me and my brothers, childless goofballs that we were?) Until her own early death by cancer in 1995, Mom would weep whenever mentioning my little cousin. I don't think she ever quite recovered from the loss, and I'm sure she wasn't alone in that.

It's almost unbearable to think of Leanne's life ending so young, of what she might have done had she lived. Just outside the room I'm staying in here at Fern's place, there is a long table holding dozens of family photos. Among them is a small photo book with Leanne's picture on the cover. I pick it up and flip through it. Leanne looks like a profoundly happy kid. Happy writers are rare. But here's the thing: if I find it nearly unbearable to meditate too long on the lost possibilities of Leanne's life, what must her mother, Fern, go through? And her sister Nirah and brother Tony.

I only know a hint of that. My brother Owen died in September 2000, while he was at home with my dad. Well, he died in the ambulance, and my poor father, himself already riddled with cancer and getting weaker, had comforted Owen while they waited for help. A stroke, a heart attack — we'll never know exactly what killed my brother at 46 (my own age right now). But I hate I hate I hate that my father had to

40

experience the loss of a child. I know he thought about Owen every day until his own death in March 2001. I know that he felt he had let Mom down; she'd left him to look after their children — me and my brothers — and he felt he'd failed. But, fighting his own battle for life, hell, he'd done his best, and my oldest brother Barry and I knew it.

So Owen is forever 46 years old, though my strongest memories of him are from when he was a teenager and we lived in the same house on Pannahill Road in Bathurst Manor. So maybe he's forever 15 for me, stomping out the door to track down the bully who had shoved me around in the schoolyard.

And Leanne is forever 11. She is an 11-year-old who wrote multiple drafts of a long short story. One of the most difficult things a writer learns is how to self-edit. How to rewrite a sentence, axe a paragraph, change a story's beginning, realize where it really ends.

Leanne was doing that at 11, where her own story ended.

October 2005

My cousin Fern now lives in Nova Scotia. She has created the Leanne Children's Foundation to help children in need have experiences in arts, sports, and recreation. She also sponsors the literary Leanne Scholarship through YouthWrite. You can find these online.

A NOVEL PUNCHED ANOTHER
NOVEL IN THE HEAD

MY BRAIN IS as disorganized as my apartment. My apartment is a mish-mash of inherited, found, and occasionally bought furniture, and every surface is cluttered with newspapers, books, manuscripts, letters, and stuffed toy monkeys. (For a smash-hit Broadway play I'm working on.) Though there is no room for anything, I continue to acquire. Like many writers — and readers — I compulsively buy more books than I could ever read in a dozen lifetimes. My bookshelves are two books deep, with more volumes crammed horizontally on top. From time to time I panic, and cart seven or eight of the books (duplicates, or maybe Stephen King, perhaps a copy of *Descant* I received at gunpoint) to my housing co-op's laundry room to put on the "Help Yourself" shelf, along with the endless Tom Clancys, outdated typing-instruction manuals, and *Know Your Dachshund.* This gives me licence to go out and buy another 40 books on a tour of Goodwills and Sally Anns conducted when I have way more pressing things to do.

This clutter and disorganization — this rabid, compulsive acquisition when I have so much to catch up on already — spills over into my publishing and my writing. Most of the successful writers I know work on one project at a time. (By successful, all I mean is that they get things finished and published and aren't a fucking mess like I am.) "I'm gonna write a novel about a guy who kidnaps Boris Karloff and then falls in love with him," they say, then they write it and send it off and it gets published and wins the Giller Prize. Then they say, "I'm going to write a sequence of poems about the liminal role of pretzels in capitalism." And they do it! They get so much *done*. It must be so clean inside their heads. You could eat perogies off the insides of their heads.

Not the insides of my head, though. I work on several projects at once, often despairing of finishing any of them. Poems accumulate in between stories, my Broadway-bound ape play, and pathetic stabs at a full-length novel that some exasperated agent somewhere is drumming his skinny little fingers about.

I can't keep the progress of my projects in my head. The other week, I felt suddenly desperate to have a book coming out sometime in the future, because I was bummed out and couldn't picture anything resembling a future. I gathered together all the poems I'd written since my last big poetry book — *Hey, Crumbling Balcony!* — came out in 2003, and saw that there were enough. Like, 80 pages. So I whittled some away, spent hours putting the remainder in some brilliant, hare-brained order whose logic no one else will be able to decipher, and sent them off to an interested publisher, hoping for the best. Over the course of the next week, more poems I'd written kept popping up as I looked for a phone bill or a curried chickpea recipe in my post-Katrina apartment.

My novel, meanwhile, has been lurching along for several years. Out of laziness, and because I'm incapable of keeping organized, I decided to write it in random chronological order, even though it takes place during about five different periods in the dishevelled protagonist's life. Oh, wait, it wasn't laziness that determined the novel's structure, I tell myself — it was that I deliberately wanted the book to take the form of a kind of quilt. Yeah, a literary quilt. The upshot is, I can barely keep track of the thing in my head: I have no way of picturing the project as a whole. Haiku are way easier (though even those can be a challenge).

A few times I've been tempted to say, "Okay, I've got 130 pages. I'll just write something really enigmatic as the ending and declare it finished." Not that there can't be good 130-page novels with enigmatic endings. In fact, those are my favourite kind, if I don't count Patricia Highsmith. But the 130 pages I've written don't add up to something finished yet. I'm not sure what's needed — exactly the right 20 additional pages, or another 100. Can it really be so arbitrary? I do know that I really want to finish this novel. This novel is important to me. It deals with things in my life that I really want to explore in my writing. It deals with my mother: she died in 1995, and I feel like I owe her this book. Not that I'm putting a lot of pressure on myself or anything.

So I was out to see a few bands the other night at Mitzi's Sister on Queen Street West, and I pulled out a little notebook. I flipped to the first clean page and printed "NOVEL" across the top. And the thing is, I wasn't solving the problems of my novel-in-progress: I was starting a *new* novel. This one, I told myself, would go really smoothly: it would proceed in chronological order, and it would have a plot — though I haven't figured one out yet — and I would write a few notebook pages a day, and I would finish it, probably within a year, which would give me plenty of time to shop for a suit for the Nobel Prize ceremony.

But here's what I'm thinking: this new novel, which I admit exists only as catharsis, will put pressure on the other novel. The other novel will have to escalate to keep up with the frisky newcomer. Then the newcomer will up the ante, threatening to pull a few pages ahead. In the end, it'll all just go back and forth between the novels, a waltz of mutually assured destruction. It'll be sort of a Cold War of novels right inside my head. The new novel is this trim young asshole, written in those short sentences that everyone's writing award-winning novels with these days. It's going to swagger up to the other novel — the old fart with its ponderous sentences that go on forever and its surreal exploration of anti-Semitism — and it's going to punch it in the head. The old novel's going to raise itself to its knees, dizzy and drooling blood, get awkwardly to its feet, brush itself off, and kick the new novel in the balls. Then kick it again. Real hard.

While those two are duking it out, smashing my furniture over each other's heads, I'm going to get back to work on my short-story collection. I'm not sure how many stories I have accumulated so far — they're all over the place — but I bet if I write another three or four and collect them all up, I'll have something. Short stories — you just need one dumb idea and you can crank out five or six pages and then the thing is done. Hell, you don't even need an idea. You just write a sentence and then you write another one after that, and soon the thing's finished and you can go cook up some chickpea curry and watch *Larry King Live*. I think his guest tonight is the guy who wrote that monkey play that's taking Broadway by storm.

June 2006

The novel I was writing became The Snowball, *and then* The Snowball and the Dragonfly, *and finally* Snowball, Dragonfly, Jew. *It took seven or eight years to write, and then ECW Press published it, in 2012. The* Globe and Mail's *A. J. Levin called it "Part Guy Maddin, part Marc Chagall, part Kurt Vonnegut, all Stuart Ross," which is pretty nice. I thought maybe it would make me a bit famous, but it didn't. I did share a prize for it, though, from the Montreal Jewish Library's J. I. Segal Awards committee: I was co-winner of the Mona Elaine*

Adilman Award for Fiction or Poetry on a Jewish Theme, which is a hell of a name for an award. But it meant a lot to me: the book is dedicated to my mother, and my mother always wanted me to be a better Jew. I mean, she wanted me to become a rabbi, but she would have settled for a better Jew.

FEAR OF THE HUNGRY BLACK HAT

SO, THE OTHER NIGHT I was carrying the black wool hat through our sparse crowd at break time, seeing how much cash I could conjure up for our two writers. It was an excellent night of readings at the Fictitious Reading Series, and the audience of about ten — smaller than usual on this cold winter night — seemed to really enjoy themselves. The third-floor gallery, donated to my co-host, Kate Sutherland, and me one evening a month by This Ain't the Rosedale Library, Toronto's greatest indie bookstore, is somewhere between a cozy living-room and a Lower East Side loft space.

The hat can be a measure of how much people value their literary experience, as compared to, say, a $13 movie or a $6 pint of beer. The first few people each happily stuffed a five or a ten into the proffered hat. The next, a girl who was very excited to attend her first reading of the series, apologized that she had no money. Really? No money at all? Okay, I guess that's possible. As I headed toward another couple, they slyly got up, headed for the long staircase down and left for the evening. Managed another couple of fivers and then headed toward the back corner for a guy who makes literature his whole life. And he makes his living — such as it is — entirely from his writing. He pushed his clenched hand into the black wool hat, and I heard the jingle of light change.

Now, when I tell people I'll be coming round with the hat, I also assure them that I won't look at what they put in, and, in fact, if they can't contribute, they can just poke their fists into the hat, and I — eyes averted, head twisted over my shoulder — won't even know the difference. I do not judge. At least, I *tell* them I do not judge.

When I was done my rounds, I scurried over to another corner of that quirky room overlooking Church Street to check out the night's take. In the bottom of the hat, beneath the bills, was about 78 cents in dimes and pennies. That'd be, um, 39 cents per reader from the guy who threw in that handful of change. Okay, so maybe Mr. Literary Life is truly broke. I poked in another eight bucks and Kate topped it up with another ten or twenty (she's a lawyer, after all), and we wound up with $36 for each reader. Not too bad, though in an ideal world they'd be getting a couple hundred bucks each for their half-hour readings plus onstage chat.

After the event, a few of us went out for drinks and some food at a corner pub in Toronto's gay ghetto, where This Ain't is located. The 78-center ordered a pint, and then he ordered another pint. I wondered if the rest of us were going to have to cover for him. But when it came time to pay, he pulled a couple of twenties out of his pocket. He tipped pretty well, too. Did he value the beer more than he valued the 60 minutes of fiction that had been read to him? Did he value the efforts of the server more than he valued the efforts of the writers?

The great American poet and painter and poetry-painter Kenneth Patchen once said, "People who say they like poetry but don't buy any are cheap sons-of-bitches." Well, yeah, Patchen was talking about poetry, but fiction that exists out of the mainstream isn't all that much different. Hell, my collection *Henry Kafka and Other Stories*, from The Mercury Press, sold far fewer copies than any of my poetry books, and that was after receiving more reviews, including a couple in the dailies. And I don't think it's because I'm a lousy fiction writer.

At the Fictitious, we don't charge admission. You walk up the stairs (hopefully after poking around and buying something at This Ain't the Rosedale Library) and you find a seat and no one charges you a cover or stamps your hand. We provide free munchies and soft drinks (Kate and I alternate making that $15 gesture each month). There is no beer to spend your money on, no wine, and no Scotch. You get two very long readings, plus an onstage interview. In all, a relaxed and absorbing two hours of exploring some pretty exciting literature. So if this guy, this guy with his handful of small change, who presents himself as a crusader for the written word, can't cough up five bucks for that experience, but he doesn't think twice about dropping six on a beer he'll soon be spraying out his wiener, then how is literature going to continue to be made? And what about that terrified young couple who escaped down the stairs, their pockets intact?

When I walked around with that black hat, I wasn't panhandling. I wasn't looking for spare change or a couple of cigarettes. I was raising money to pay the writers. I was giving the audience the opportunity to show their appreciation in a tangible way that would help put food on table, roof above head, paper in printer.

But maybe whining about moolah is inappropriate. Certainly peering into the hat and seeing what someone dropped in (and then writing a column about it) was completely inappropriate. Especially after I specifically announced I wouldn't do that. I had said emphatically, "I won't look!"

But where does this attitude — held by some, certainly some at every installment of the Fictitious Reading Series — come from, that beer and CDs and taxis and burgers are all worth money, but art isn't? That writers at a reading are just some kinda performing monkeys who don't need to be paid? Who should simply be grateful to have an audience?

So here are my demands. You will come to the next Fictitious Reading. You will bring your own beer, thus saving you about eight bucks on two of them, compared to what you'd pay at a bar for a couple of pints, badly poured. When the black hat comes and looks deep into your eyes, deep into your soul, deep into the horrible extremes of your macaroni-and-cheese-filled bowels, you will place those eight stinking dollars into its grateful, woolly embrace. Then I will hand each of the writers four dollars on your behalf. Canadian literature will be saved. No writer shall go hungry or without a roof over her noggin.

Thing is, though, the writers have never complained about their take from the door. They're always pleasantly surprised — they weren't expecting anything, so what the hell am I talking about? Well, it's a matter of conditioning. We writers are so goddamn used to not making any money from our writing that we're grateful for the 39 cents. Hey, someone cared! Someone sacrificed the price of a BiC disposable razor! In exchange for my writing, they will go unshaved! The wool from their sweater will catch on their chin bristles as they pull it over their head.

Friend, we have some new rules now. The black hat awaits you.

November 2006

So far as I know, the Fictitious Reading Series was the only all-fiction event of its kind in Toronto history until Words at the Wise started up in 2014. The nights were long: Kate and I asked the readers to go for up to 40 minutes, and afterwards, after the break, during which few people bailed (unless they feared the black hat), either Kate or I — she was better at it, really — hosted an "onstage" discussion with the two guest writers, and invited questions and comments from the audience. The series lasted close to two years. We hosted Lynn Coady, Clint Burnham, John Lavery, Derek McCormack, Marianne Apostolides, Maggie Helwig, John Degen, Marnie Woodrow, Elyse Friedman, and plenty more. Helluva series.

On the subject of hats, let me boast a bit, okay? It is because of me that the Pivot Reading Series takes a collection for the writers, and it is because of me that the writers get a couple of free drinks, courtesy of the Press Club (the bar at which the series is held). Once upon a time, I was doing a reading at Pivot's predecessor, the I.V. Lounge Reading Series. The place was filled up with people buying drinks. So when I got up to the bar to read, the manager was in a back room, maybe the kitchen, and I said really loudly, "So the writers fill up the place with people who buy drinks, and we don't even get a free drink ourselves?" Series organizer and awesome poet Paul Vermeersch rushed up and offered to buy me a drink. I turned him down; I didn't think it should come out of his pocket. And after a bit more loud complaining, I did my reading. After that night, the I.V. Lounge always ponied up a couple of drinks for the writer. That series became Pivot when Paul moved it to the Press Club.

And then when I was invited to read at the Pivot series — I think it was Jacob McArthur Mooney, the current organizer who asked me — I told him, "Look, I have to come in all the way from Cobourg. Could you pass a hat for me to help cover some travel funds?" He didn't think it would be fair to pass the hat for only one of the writers, so he did pass a hat, and divvied it up between the three writers presenting their work, and has done so ever since.

ONE MUSE, PLEASE, WITH EXTRA PEPPERONI

YOU KNOW WHAT really bugs me? I'm at some awful reading, and I've wound up — against my will — at a table where a bunch of writers I don't know are sitting, and they're the kind of writers who are writing their own poems during the open mic, waiting for their own turns up there in front of the audience, and in the course of their chatter, because they're chattering while they're writing, someone says either "I haven't found my voice yet," or "I've got writer's block and it's really frustrating," or maybe something hideous like "I'm waiting for my muse."

These three things — the muse, writer's block, and the elusive voice — are the Great Lies of the writing industry, or maybe of the teaching-writing industry. I mean, for god's sake, just sit down and write. Or sit down and read. Read some Larry Eigner — now, there was a guy who was confronted by barriers to writing (palsied since childhood, he could type only with his right index finger and thumb) and he bashed them down with his wheelchair and wrote books and books of beautiful and unsettling poetry. Really, just read *anyone*. Then pick up a pen, or plant yourself in front of a screen, and start writing. Forget all this mystical crap. There's nothing sacred involved in hammering out a poem or a story.

First, this whole concept of finding one's "voice." What does it mean exactly? What it often ends up meaning is that someone is trying their hardest to write in Lorna Crozier's voice, or Charles Bukowski's. But they don't say, "I'm trying to find Charles Bukowski's voice." Or maybe they're looking for Anne Carson's voice. There are an awful lot of people looking for Anne Carson's voice these days. I think it might have fallen behind the fridge. Ron Padgett says when he hears that someone is trying to find their voice, he assumes they mean the latest issue of the *Village Voice*.

Look, you read 400 poetry books, you scrawl some poems — morning, noon, or night; while you're in your kitchen, in the bathtub, on the subway, in the bank lineup, at your government job writing amendments to drivers' licensing manuals — and what you write is your voice. That's it. It's your voice. Give it a hug and get it over with and get writing. And maybe your voice changes every six months or every six years, maybe every couple of decades. You'd better hope it does, or you'll end up like poor Charles Bukowski, whose poems pretty much never changed. He lived for 150 years and never developed as a poet. I mean, who can really read more than two or three books by that guy?

And when the word "muse" comes up in my workshops, I feel like grabbing for the fly-swatter. Maybe it's just me, but when I think of "muse," I think of some pale and lovely ethereal Elizabethan boy or girl, draped in robes or wrapped in giant tea doilies, floating through an open window to the flutterings of a harp (played by another muse). The muse alights on the struggling writer's shoulder, emitting the scent of lavender or perhaps pickle juice, and whispers sweet nothings into the writer's ear, and the writer's eyes begin to slowly widen and some horrible piece of crap gets written.

The muse, according to scientific studies, is most often invoked when the writer hasn't written anything for ages. "I'm still looking for my muse." "My muse hasn't visited in so long!" "I saw a guy who looked like my muse on the Bathurst bus, but it turned out to be Nibbles Horowitz, who I went to high school with." "I ordered a voice from my muse, but she hasn't delivered it yet."

The best muse around is heaving your goddamn Natalie Goldberg book out the window and killing a passing crow with it. Perhaps the perfect replacement for that copy of *Writing Down the Bones* that's now quivering on the sidewalk below, being trampled by oblivious passersby, is Joe Brainard's *I Remember*, any edition you can get your hands on. Now, there's a book you can live with for an entire lifetime, and a book that can spark a lifetime's worth of writing.

Of course, this all ties into writer's block, which is the biggest farce of all, a non-existent industry that probably sells tens of thousands of books published by Writer's Digest. I propose this: if you have writer's block, you're not a writer. Am I being too harsh? I mean, first you say you're too depressed to write, and then you say you can't write unless you're depressed.

That's not to say you're not going to have three months or two years when you don't write anything that wouldn't be better off crumpled up and flung into the fireplace. Or, like Henry Roth, you write the greatest American novel ever in 1930 and then you take a cigarette break till 1990 and write a couple of trilogies. This thing of not writing is an integral part of writing. Eventually, you're going to write again, so long as you don't contract some biological-weapon virus or kill yourself before it happens (and these risks are both very common among writers).

And you *can* write. You just tap the keys on your keyboard or you drag a pen across a piece of paper. You babble stuff to your voice-recognition software. You write the word "eggplant" and then you write the word "oof!" There you go: two real good words, and a cross-lingual pun thrown in for good measure. Or you copy out a poem by Emily Dickinson and then re-place all the nouns with names of Ikea futon-beds and win the Pulitzer Prize.

Or you read. I mentioned that before, but it's important, so I'll mention it again, which will also help to make this book longer. Because reading is writing. *Someone* said that. Probably a lot of people did. I'm sure one of them was Ted Berrigan, but maybe Eddie Money said it too, and Golda Meir, back when she was a Beat.

When I don't write for a long time, it's not because I have writer's block. It's not because the muse hasn't come fox-trotting through my screen door lately. Not because I just, darn it, haven't found my voice yet.

If I don't write for a long time, it's because I'm a lazy sack of shit. There're no two ways about it. And, really, it's way easier to watch *South Park* than to write a poem or finish a novel or start a short story. In fact, it's easier to do just about anything than it is to write. It's certainly easier to talk about writing than it is to write.

It's easier to put on a beret, grow a goatee, sit in a café with some Rimbaud or Nick Cave book displayed on the table, or a copy of Buk's *Post Office* chasing gerbils around in your butt, than it is to write. It's easier to sit in that café and tell the cowering legal secretary at the next table, who's just trying to get through her copy of some Ann Quin novel, "I've written a book, but it's all up here, in my head. I've just got to put it down on paper now."

On the other hand, it's easier to write than to make goddamn lattes all day for people with berets and goatees.

April 2007

THE BOOKS THAT SHAPED AND DESTROYED ME

WHEN I WAS a teenager, I worked in a library up at Bathurst and Lawrence, starting at $1.45 an hour. I was surrounded by books. And after school, or sometimes instead of school, Mark Laba and I headed downtown for the 85-cent lunch special at Kwong Chow, followed by an exhilarating sweep of the used bookstores on Queen Street; there were a lot of them between University and Spadina, led by the legendary Village Bookstore. Then we headed a couple of blocks south to the sprawling indoor football field of books that was Old Favourites, which had a five-cent Coke machine and a lot of musty volumes we weren't really interested in. But we loved the mustiness, the bookness, the ancientness of the guy behind the cash desk. If we were done early enough, we might head back up to Harbord Street, where Paul Stuewe ran Nth Hand, definitely the coolest bookstore in the city, and Paul always knew what books to lay on us. It was also the only place in Toronto you could get the latest issue of *3¢ Pulp*, the often-single-sheet magazine published by Vancouver's mythical Pulp Press, fine purveyors of literary terrorism.

Now, three decades later, as I'm on the cusp of living under a bridge and eating dog food (no academic credentials and can't stomach taking another regular job), I return to some of the books I bought as a teenager:

the novels that are to blame for my impending decline. The ones that confirmed my desire to be a writer. I've still got them all. Sometimes more than one copy, because I can't resist buying them again when I find them in used bookstores or thrift shops.

And it's the perfect time to talk about the novels of my adolescence, because I recently finished my own first novel. If it gets published, I stand to make a thousand bucks, or maybe two thousand. None of this $500 crap you might earn on a poetry book. Novels are the big time.

As a little kid, it was the Hardy Boys for me, the Black Stallion, Henry Huggins, or maybe it was Higgins — the guy with the big doughnut-making machine anyway — and those warped little futuristic books by John Christopher about teens enslaved by alien tripods. Maybe a John Wyndham. Or Oscar, that seal who took on Nazi U-boats single finnedly. What a fuckin' tremendous, anti-fascist seal.

But then suddenly I was post-bar mitzvah and I made the leap to books for grown-ups. After all, I had just sung for 15 minutes in a language I didn't understand in front of 250 people in a synagogue. One of the first adult books I read was Dalton Trumbo's anti-war masterpiece, *johnny got his gun*, which'd been first published in 1939. It blew my mind and it shaped me. Joe, wounded in battle, is lying in a hospital bed. He has no arms, no legs, no face. And we are stuck inside his head. Which he taps on the pillow in Morse code to try to communicate. I read this book over and over. I couldn't believe how the simple, declarative sentences of the first 180 pages shifted into nearly punctuationless, run-on rants in the heavy-handed but brilliant last few pages: "He saw a world of armless mothers clasping headless babies to their breasts trying to scream out their grief from throats that were cancerous with gas." Roll over, Stephen Crane, and tell Erich Maria-Remarque the news.

The French writer and artist Roland Topor also blew my teenage mind.

He made me shudder and made me laugh with *The Tenant* (1966), one of the greatest literary explosions of paranoia, and *Joko's Anniversary* (1970), still among the strangest novels I've read, and I've read some fucked-up specimens. Eager to make a little extra cash, Joko starts carrying people around on his back, a kind of human taxi. Then things go horribly wrong, and one by one his customers become stuck to his back, adhered there by a mysterious goop. Soon the guy has seven permanent passengers: "They had fallen asleep, strewn all over the bed like broken skittles. From time to time, in his dream, Sir Barnett let fly with a kick in Joko's chest. Joko wasn't asleep. He was thinking of Wanda. She was so close, and practically naked."

Much blood and sawing ensues.

I don't remember an awful lot about *The Weekend Man*, Richard B. Wright's second novel, also from 1970, but I read it, and Mark Laba read it, and we made our friend David Fine read it. I think it was about an ad man, suburbs, and a strained marriage. But I remember it as dark and subtly weird. Somehow it appealed to us teenagers. And then all three of us read *The Fan Man* (1974) — a book as celebratorily bizarre as its author's name: William Kotzwinkle. Actually, I read the whole thing to Dave over the phone, I'm pretty sure. We'd never read anything like it: Horse Badorties, rancid hippie, seeks out 15-year-old girls to join his Love Chorus. The book is one extended monologue, punctuated every fifth word with "man." And there's an entire chapter that consists of just the word "dorky," repeated over and over again for several glorious pages. I was about 15 when I read this book for the first time, and I didn't realize how inappropriate it was for Horse to be bringing girls my age back to his love pad, where he'd cool them off with a battery-operated handheld fan.

Options, by the science-fiction writer Robert Sheckley, was a huge influence. A couple of the chapters last only one or two sentences. I loved that that was possible. This book was unlike any other science-fiction novel I'd ever read. It made Robert Heinlein sound like Robert Ludlum. Reading it was the closest I've ever gotten to dropping acid.

And then I became obsessed with Mervyn Peake, whose *Mr. Pye* (1953) was a demented tale of good and evil about a bald, rotund old dude in a derby who attempts to spread good on a tiny island populated by oddballs. Peake, who in addition to writing fiction was also a great artist and extremely strange poet, died slowly and excruciatingly from Parkinson's and encephalitis as he raced to finish his gloomy, magnificent *Gormenghast Trilogy*. Among his notes were plans to make an opera of the thing, too. I also read a couple of memoirs of Mervyn, by his wife, Maeve Gilmore, and his son Sebastian, but I think that was a few years later.

My own novel is tiny, about 140 pages, and perhaps the first tiny novel for grown-ups I read was Günter Grass's *Cat and Mouse* (1963), a dark and grotesque tale of a sordid adolescence, set in Nazi Germany. Our young heroes have wanking contests, spurting their copious splooge off a rusty bridge onto a passing torpedo boat below. The winner was invariably Mahlkie, who also ate dried pigeon shit he scraped off the bridge: "The stuff tasted of nothing at all or like plaster or like fish meal or like everything imaginable: happiness, girls, God in His heaven."

After these literary freaks, Beckett, Vonnegut, Highsmith, Kosinski, and B. S. Johnson — the master — were just a little ways down the road.

Mark is the restaurant reviewer for the Vancouver *Province* now and Dave is an Oscar-winning animator. Me, I'm looking for a comfortable cardboard box to settle down in and nail my second novel over a bowl of Alpo.

January 2008
Mark is no longer at the Province. *He is Canada's greatest underpublished*

literary genius and the prolific madman behind the blog The Haltiwanger Report, whose influences, no doubt, include some of the discoveries from our teenage days. It's practically a part-time job for me to wrench manuscripts out of Mark and try to find publishers for them.

UP SINCE 5:30, DOWN SINCE 1959

ARE ALL WRITERS as negative and self-loathing as me? Is there even a single writer with a sunny disposition who greets the morning, pressing her face into the flood of warm sunlight that gushes through her bedroom window, and chirps, "Oh, glorious life! I can't wait to write!"

Me, I wake up slowly, groggily, reluctantly, eyes burning, always far too early, no matter what insomnia-driven time I get to sleep, and within seconds there's the foggy realization of who I am and the sorry circumstances of my life, and I feel despondency set in. And while it's true I don't live in a lean-to made of rusting, battered automobile hoods in a garbage dump on the outskirts of Managua, Nicaragua, I still somehow feel justified in whining. I lie on my back on my book- and paper-strewn bed and stare at the cobwebs dangling from my ceiling and quietly murmur, "I can't wait to see how I avoid writing today. I'm more than halfway through my life and I haven't accomplished a goddamn thing."

Now, it can be scientifically determined that I have had five full-length poetry collections published, a book each of short stories and personal essays, a couple of collaborative novellas, and a heap of chapbooks. My last poetry book, *I Cut My Finger*, received rave reviews across the board, even in *The Globe & Mail* and *The Toronto Star*. Also, the excellent Montreal poet Jason Camlot, on taking the helm of a new imprint of DC Books called Punchy Poetry, contacted me and said he wanted the first title he put out to be by me. I'd just had a book out, its corpse not even cold yet, but I rustled together an insane new manuscript called *Dead Cars in Managua*, and Jason fell for it.

But this isn't enough to make me love myself.

A cursory investigation would also show that over the past year and a bit, I have had the opportunity to edit books by four of my poetry heroes — guys who shook my world when I was real young, and whose works have been vital to me ever since. Through my own Proper Tales Press, I published *If I Were You*, a collection of poems Ron Padgett wrote collaboratively with the likes of Allen Ginsberg, Ted Berrigan, Alice Notley, and James Schuyler. Also through Tales, I put out the chapbook *Concrete Sky*, 15 haiku all beginning with the same line, by Tom Walmsley, with an assist from Michael Healey's donated liver.

Through Insomniac Press, I edited and introduced a 300-plus-page collection called *Why Are You So Sad? Selected Poems of David W. McFadden*, which may be the best book in the history of Canadian poetry. In fact, it is one of three books shortlisted for the Canadian 2008 Griffin Poetry Prize, and if it wins, Dave might pay for my next order of French fries at Legends, our divey go-to bar on St. Clair West. Most recently, as poetry editor for Mansfield Press, I edited a book called *Dog*, written by poets Joe Rosenblatt and Catherine Owen, based on photos by Karen Moe. Even though Joe flipped through about 50 of my poems, back when I was in high school, and muttered "Nothing worth salvaging here," he is a hero of mine, and now I've edited one of his books.

But this isn't enough, either.

Here are two other things that just aren't enough. When the current coordinators of the Toronto Small Press Book Fair (an institution I co-founded a couple of decades ago) hired a lawyer to threaten me with a defamation suit because they didn't like my harsh but constructive criticism of the [CENSORED] job they did coordinating the fair, I received scores of letters of support, and they, reportedly, received upward of a hundred letters of condemnation; I mean, what the hell are a couple of writers doing threatening another writer with a defamation suit? Good fucking gawd. Anyway, I've had so many people try to comfort me by saying stuff along the lines of, "Look, neither of *them* will ever write a poem as good as your worst poem." And while that may be true, it isn't really the point.

Oh yeah — the other thing. My friend Ben Walker, who is a brilliant British singer/songwriter, and the son of Colin Ward, one of the world's most famous anarchist thinkers, and also the step-grandson of Bertrand Russell, recorded a whole CD's worth of songs he built around my poems. He and I jointly released it as *An Orphan's Song: Ben Walker Sings Stuart Ross* (send me a 20 and I'll send you a copy). It was perhaps the greatest compliment my poetry has ever been paid.

But, you see, I am a self-pitying jerk, so it's still not enough to make me greet the morning with burbling enthusiasm.

If this sounds like the kind of inventory one compiles before one kills oneself, you're in no such luck. You wish I'd abandon this last page of *sub-Terrain* so that Karen Connelly could take over and write about Far More Important Things, but you'll have to pry this page from my cold dead hands. Not that I'm going to kill myself, mind you. I don't have the heart to sentence anyone to the task of dealing with the bubbling archaeological morass that is my apartment. Plus, I'll do everything in my power — including not killing myself — to stop Karen Connelly from taking over this page.

When I moan about my sorry personal life, about the hurt I've caused, about the endless regrets I carry, the lack of family, the chaos of my home (my entire apartment looks like the walk-in closet of some lunatic who has kept clippings of every newspaper article that contained the word "the" for 40 years) — when I moan about this stuff, my spectacular friends — and my friends *are* spectacular, I'm blessed that way — tell me I'm a good guy, and a good writer, and I inspire lots of other writers, and also I don't live in a garbage dump in Central America.

But this isn't enough. I'd give up the whole writing thing in exchange for a life of serenity and self-acceptance.

April 2008

This whining column earned me the only mention I'll ever get in the New York Times Book Review — or, at least, its associated ArtsBeat blog. ". . . I'll pick up subTerrain again, not least for its prickly back page column, called Hunkamooga," wrote Dwight Garner. Subby publisher Brian Kaufman was so happy that his mag made the NYTBR blog that he sent me down to New York City for two years in a row to represent the mag and Anvil at the Indie and Small Press Book Fair. So that was pretty neat. But soon thereafter the fair imploded; attendance was becoming increasingly dismal and many of the most important publishers, I guess, were uninterested in taking part.

For me, the best part of it all was meeting Karen Brissette, Goodreads' #1 reviewer and, at the time, a buyer for Barnes & Noble. She's a big fan of a lot of Canadian writers, and was excited to see a new Canadian publisher at the fair. We became pals. I also met avant-gardist legend Richard Kostelanetz (who recently asked to be removed from my New Year's poem email list, because my poetry sucks), poet Sarah Sarai, novelist Rob Stephenson, Brissette co-conspirator Greg Stahl, and probably some more people I can't remember.

LIVE SEX AND
AIR-CONDITIONER REPAIR

IT'S TOUGH TO decide what to grouse about this time: the Spoken Word Pandemic or Open Mic Disease. I mean, they're related. One of the causes of both of these terrifying afflictions is Blind Encouragement of Shit. Another cause is a seeming disdain for reading contemporary poetry, and an insistence on exposing oneself only to other open mikers or other spoken worders.

I sat through another open mic set last night at the Art Bar Poetry Series in Toronto. Why do I repeatedly put myself through such punishment? I went to hear one of the "features" (Gawd, I hate that word! And it's pretty much used only at series that have open mics), and she was on third, and immediately thereafter the open mic began. Why did I stay? Why do the feature readers sit through them? Are any of us paid enough for such waterboarding? I think we're just too goddamn nice to slap down the money for our pint, get up, and walk out the door.

Oh yeah, and the other week I was at the Plasticine Poetry Series, because I wanted to hear Paul Vermeersch read. Then Carey Toane, a really good young poet, was going to read in the open mic, because occasionally that happens: someone good reads at an open mic. You know, you're stringing up a noose to hang yourself from the rotating fan on the ceiling, in the clouds above the bar the vultures are circling, and suddenly you hear a couple of lines that indicate that the reader has actually read, oh, I dunno: John Ashbery? Karen Solie? Wislawa Szymborska? So, okay, I figured I'd stick around. But get this: just before the open mic begins, a few of these spoken wordy characters come slinking in. They've missed the "features," but they've clearly just read at the Art Bar open mic down the street, and now they want to inflict their narcissistic ramblings on yet another audience. (Carey was great, mind you.)

And who reads the most dreadful abominations at these open mics? It's the spoken worders, the slammers — the "air poets." It killed me the first time I heard them call writers like me "page poets." Anyway, they pontificate that they are following in the tradition of oral writers like Homer and Billy Shakespeare. And then they recite stuff like: "Poetry is great, it's my freight, it gets me dates..." Okay, I just made that up. Let's see how a master does it, like Tomy Bewick, in his poem "Do You 'Fro?": "Do I 'fro? / How am I supposed to know? / I'm white, and I don't have an afro. / Mind you, I do have a flow / And to be honest I'm always attempting to progress spiritually as I grow." Clever AAAAA rhyme scheme. Someone call AAAAA Towing Company to drag this guy off the stage!

And then there's all that spoken word stuff that's in-your-face political and social-consciousnessy. Godawful, didactic two-by-fours by people who have clearly not taken "show, don't tell" to heart. An opinion, stated loudly, dramatically, and in rhyme, is not literature. This is the lesson spoken word seems incapable of absorbing. Spoken word lacks subtlety, lacks nuance, and most of the time lacks imagery. It certainly lacks word play, except for rhymes and puns, typically delivered with a raised eyebrow and a "Do you get it?" glance, head tilted suggestively.

I'm probably lucky I live in Toronto, as opposed to "The Most

66

Beautiful Place in the Milky Way Solar System," because I get the idea that Vancouver is practically run by spoken worders, just like Montreal. Even the language poets, whose empire crumbled after the '80s, have to meet in secret and try to pass in public, with a Shane Koyczan book tucked under their arms. (It's really just a Koyczan cover wrapped around a Billy Collins cover wrapped around a Lisa Robertson book. Don't worry.) But even here in Toronto, as Vermeersch pointed out on his blog not long ago, there seems to be this movement among the series organizers that an air poet has to be included in every reading, because just having page poets would be elitist. So I go to see Jenny Sampirisi and Jenn LoveGrove read, and I have to sit through Valentino Assenza. (Actually, I went out onto the bar's patio for most of his time onstage and took up smoking.) And a guy there asked me if I would "feature" at his reading out on the Danforth. I said yeah, but then decided that when he emails me the confirmation, I'll make it a condition that there are no slammers on the bill, because I really don't want to subject my friends to that. Besides, when was the last time George Bowering or Alice Burdick were invited to read at a spoken word event?

Poetry and spoken word on one bill. It's sort of like selling seats for a football and crocheting event. Or a live sex show with a lecture on air-conditioner repair. Can anyone be a fan of both of these things?

Okay, but back to open mics. I think there's this misguided theory that poetry should be democratic, and open mics are somehow democratic. But what other art form pairs up people who haven't studied the art form with people who take it seriously? Film doesn't do it, nor dance, nor video installation, nor classical music. There's no room at the AGO where they put up paintings by Charles Pachter and Shary Boyle and then fill a corner with go-go-dancing kittens and stick figures with angel wings.

Of course, there are exceptions. There are talented writers, like Ali

Riley, Clifton Joseph, Sandra Alland, and Lillian Allen, who manage to straddle the two worlds, but I usually prefer their work on the page, anyway. And, like I said, there is the occasional gem in the open-mic set. But if I consider the hundreds of hours of my life I've spent in the presence of open mics, I weep. I might as well wait for those gems to get published and read them on the page, instead of suffering through the battalion of earnestness and misplaced ego.

And this is the worst part — this is the part that makes me sit literary shiva — the crappier the open-mic poet is, the greater the applause: because the applause is compassion and encouragement, rather than reward for good writing. "Aw, she tried so hard!" "That was straight from the heart!" "He really misses his grandmother and her cat!" And when I hear the spoken word fans cheer on the guy reading "Poverty Sucks," I think, "Okay, there are all these people who like it. Does that mean it's good?" Then I remember I live in a society where McDonald's gets voted the Best Fucking Hamburger in "progressive" entertainment weeklies' Best of the City polls.

When I started writing this column (about 20 minutes ago), I thought to myself, "If I publish this, all these spoken word people are gonna boycott my books." Then I realized I didn't have to worry: they don't actually read poetry.

August 2008

HOW JEW YOU DO?

WHEN I TRAVEL to smaller towns — like New Denver or Invermere in the Kootenays; Lethbridge, Alberta; Wolfville, Nova Scotia; Cobourg, Ontario — to do readings or lead workshops, I am aware there aren't a lot of Jews around. Maybe I'm the only one. Maybe people in these minuscule places have never seen a Jew, and it's not their fault. Maybe they don't even realize I'm a Jew when they look at me. Does being a Jew in a place without Jews make me exotic or Other? In fact, I don't even know what the Jewish population of any of these places is, so maybe I'm just full of shit and making stupid assumptions.

Now, I'm practically entirely unreligious, though I identify strongly as a Jew, and I live with the awareness that most of my grandparents' brothers and sisters died at the hands of Nazis. It's tough not to imagine what might have happened if Max and Sarah Razovsky and Sam and Nina Blatt hadn't come to Canada before the 1930s. I likely wouldn't exist. Perhaps my parents would have existed, and likely they would have found themselves in concentration camps. I read Cynthia Ozick's short story "The Shawl" over and over, because it is a nearly perfect piece of writing and because it so effectively and brilliantly evokes the most horrific chapter in Jewish history.

So there I am in a bar in Cobourg — a town that, despite its name, is not a partner in the law firm Goldberg, Rosenberg & Fischbaum — or maybe a bar in Lethbridge, the Sudbury of Alberta, and I'm standing in front of an audience of strangers, and I find myself faced with two conflicting impulses: read stuff with Jewish content or don't read stuff with Jewish content.

Although in the past decade (perhaps since the death of my mother, Shirley, in 1995, followed too soon by my brother Owen and my dad, Sydney), Jewish stuff has begun to permeate some of my writing, it's not a real big part of my work over the past 30 years if you add everything up. My childhood buddy and still-buddy Mark Laba, on the other hand — he's like the Henny Youngman of contemporary Canadian poetry: his work is equal parts Yiddish vaudeville and surrealist/Dadaist. Even his every-Thursday restaurant column in the Vancouver *Province* sounds like something you'd hear at a Catskills resort in 1964. Me, I'm no Stanley Elkin, no Bruce Jay Friedman. For sure no Philip Roth.

Still, I'm frustrated that I don't get invited to read at the Toronto Jewish Book Fair and that my books are always ignored by the *Canadian Jewish News*. Well, okay, Hal Niedzviecki once booked me for the Ashkenaz Festival of Yiddish Culture in Toronto. And the Vancouver Jewish Community Centre brought me to read for a Hebrew day school last year. (When I read at Books & Bagels at the Toronto JCC once, they'd double-booked the room with a talk on Jewish Burial Practices, and by the puzzled look on many of the faces in the audience, I think their corrective signage wasn't very effective.) And a few years back, I got to read at the Jewish Book Fair in Vancouver, along with my buddy Elyse Friedman and Hal. Chaim Potok kicked off that festival, which I think was his last public appearance. He was ancient and rambling, but passionate and defiant, as he was interviewed onstage, giving some very surreal answers to which the mostly older, upscale audience nodded knowingly, maybe figuring that Potok was just being real deep.

Potok was there to launch his book, a collection of short stories with a brilliantly evocative title: *Old Men at Midnight.* When I was a kid, I read some of his classic early novels: *The Chosen* and *My Name Is Asher Lev* among them. Every Jewish household in North York had some of those on the shelves. I loved those books about conflicted pimply Jewish youths. They didn't get to touch forbidden girls' nipples down in the basement like the kids in Harold Robbins' novels. They didn't even get to date a slab of liver, like Alexander Portnoy.

Oh, right, so there I am in no-Jew's-land, shuffling neurotically through my papers and books before a reading. I always go through this ritual, no matter where I am, because how can I know what to read before I'm in the room where I'm going to read? Anyway, one part of me wants to declare myself a Jew there, and maybe offer up a new experience for those in the room who might not have rubbed shoulders lately with Barbra Streisand, Sammy Davis Jr. or Shylock. But such an impulse is immediately countered by a fear of being an exhibitionist or being a strident Jew, whatever that is, and providing a target for anti-Semites.

So I decide to read my poem "After the Shiva." Do I tell them what a "shiva" is? If it wasn't a religious word — for example, if it was the word "spelunk" — would I tell them what it means then? "I'm gonna read this poem called 'After the Shiva.' A shiva is this thing where, after someone Jewish dies, the family of the person who died stay in their house or apartment for about a week, and they take the cushions off the sofas and paint the mirrors with white paint, and then people come and visit them and bring them food and kibbitz — "

"Excuse me, is 'kibbitz' that farm kinda place where people in Israel go to live collectively?"

"No, that's 'kibbutz.' 'Kibbitz' is where you give someone the business, you know, you tell jokes, you shoot the shit. So, people come over and they chat and console the mourners, and they have, like, this whole schedule about when people are bringing the mourners meals, because the mourners aren't supposed to cook…"

Oh yeah, there was a poem to read. I skip the explanation. I try to look really Jewish so maybe they get the idea that I'm saying something Jewish-related when I say "shiva" and maybe they can figure out the word given its context. I feel like a show-off. I know I'm desperate to declare my identity in a place where my identity isn't even on the radar. I wish my grandparents hadn't changed our name from Razovsky to Ross. With a label like Razovsky on me, I wouldn't feel such an intense need to declare myself.

On my way out after the reading, which actually goes over pretty well — there have been no conversions or circumcisions, but no pogroms either — someone wishes me a Merry Christmas.

December 2008

A year or two after this column was published, I moved to Cobourg. When Passover rolled around, I went to the local grocery store, hoping against hope I could find a box of matzoh, but feeling deep down that it was futile. Lo and behold, after a long search, the hundreds of bags of white bread parted, and there, at the end of the bakery aisle, were a couple of boxes of Streit's up on a top shelf. I grabbed one and headed toward the cash register. As I was approaching, a woman who looked not unlike someone I might have sat next to at a Toronto synagogue, saw what I was carrying, then yelled to a guy who was going through checkout, "Look, there's another one here!" I never saw my Jewish Cobourg friends again, but I knew then that I wasn't alone.

FLASH GORDON MEETS THE
LONG-NECKED STAPLER

I AM 89 years old, lying in a hospital bed, and there are tubes coming out of my nose. Otherwise, I'm doing pretty good, thank you. People are colonizing Neptune and creating an uncompromised socialist utopia there, but I've decided to stay back on Earth, because I hate moving. My newest trade book, *Even Still More Goddamn Further Endless Whiny Confessions of a Small Press Racketeer*, is sitting by my bedside. It's printed on a shaved gerbil or readable on a wrist-computer or digestible as a fennel-flavoured capsule or whatever the technology for books is in 2049.

But I've got one of those food trays hovering over my belly (that's right, they actually hover in the mid-21st century), and on it are several small stacks of paper and a long-necked stapler. It takes a lot of energy, and I sure don't have much at this point, but I'm folding and stapling my new poetry chapbook. It's called *Skip & Biff Cling to the Radio*. I did a chapbook with the exact same title back in 1984, but I've long forgotten. The poems in this one are different anyway. I've been writing for about 75 years and I've improved marginally. I'm still not quite where I want to be as a poet, but there's a bit of time still. A bit.

I've just assembled the first copy of the chapbook and I'm putting a couple of staples into the spine. I tell the nurse I'm "horse-stitching" my new chapbook, but I mean "saddle-stitching." Every word in every poem in the chapbook is a word I used instead of the word I meant. I've become famous for this, for Meantist Poetry, and I've finally won the Governor General's Award, for my 2036 collection, *Razovsky Goes Bowling with the Oddfellows*, which was issued in both hardcover *and* soft-cover gerbil.

The first copy of a new chapbook still excites me. I slowly flip through the pages, admiring how badly I've folded them. I admire the title page, the colophon, the typography of each page of poetry. I read the little author bio in the back and admire the author photo, taken when I was 63. I press the booklet flat on the food tray, and with one wrinkled, bony finger, I smooth out the spine. It makes the books easier to stack that way. It feels satisfying.

The first chapbook I ever made was called *He Counted His Fingers, He Counted His Toes*, back in 1979. Somehow, it permeates my foggy brain that this is the 70th anniversary of my small press, Proper Tales. I am giddy for about one-sixth of a second — that's all the strength I have for giddiness. Twenty-three skidoo. I ask the nurse to hand me the phone and I call up David W. McFadden. He's about 109 and he's still never won the Governor General's Award, even though he's Canada's greatest poet. Raymond Souster, who is in his early 300s and has recently released his 19th volume of selected poems, always makes fun of David about that. Margaret Atwood, who created a gizmo to autograph her books remote-ly, hasn't even been *shortlisted* for the GG a single time since she created that gizmo to write her *poems* remotely. The gizmo keeps winding up on the GG jury and there's some kinda big hullabaloo about conflict of interest.

David congratulates me on the anniversary of Proper Tales Press and tells me that he's just finished a sequence of 700 sestinas about abstract expressionist painter Barnett Newman. I promise to help him get it published and we agree to meet for a celebratory pint at Legends, where they have a framed photo of Mickey Rooney on the wall. I'm thinking I might need a celebratory pint of blood.

No matter how long I've been at this game, I never get sick of chapbooks. I remember back to 2008, the year before the 30th anniversary of Proper Tales Press, celebrated in the opening months of the Great Holy Shit Depression, the one that marked the collaborative annexation of the desiccated United States by Canada and Nicaragua. Me and eight other small pressers started a collective called Meet the Presses, and we put on our first Indie Literary Market, and a couple of days before the event I figured I needed to publish something new. Time was tight, so I came up with a very simple format: a tiny chapbook, a quarter the size of a piece of letter-size paper, with a basic text-only cover. Each chapbook contained a short story: one was called *The Twelve Rabbis of, Um, of, Uh . . .* and the other was called *So Sue Me, You Talentless Fucker.*

These two were the most basic chapbooks I'd ever created, and I was thrilled with them, thrilled with the absence of ornamentation, thrilled I could sell each of these 12- to 16-pagers for just a toonie. Somehow they were even more fulfilling than any of my "real" books. And that's still the way it is 40 years later. No matter how many handsome gerbils with my name printed on their spines I have lined up on my sagging bookshelf, or how many fennel-flavoured text capsules, I still get real excited about far more ephemeral publications.

Back to my hospital bed, though. Occasionally some of the young writers come to visit me. First, I make them buy a chapbook, the cheap bastards. This is an important discipline for them, and a nearly lost art. Then I ask them what they're working on. Inevitably, it's some post-post-post-post-fucking-blah-blah-blah long poem, and they're hoping to go straight to gerbil with one of the big literary presses. They will never know the joys of scoring and folding a chapbook cover. They will never horse-stitch.

I'm tired, but need to read a bit before sleeping. I buzz the nurse and ask him to hand me the licorice-flavoured capsule on the bedside table, plus a cup of water (flown in from some other goddamn solar system where they still have water). This capsule is the new poetry collection by Lisa Jarnot. She just keeps getting better. The new capsule is even more amazing than the last capsule. My eyelids become heavy, and the chapbooks slide off my hovering food table, tumble over my blankets, and land silently on the floor.

January 2009

MAKE MINE MISCELLANEOUS!

EARLIER THIS YEAR, I sat on a jury for the Canada Council for the Arts. We were giving out grants for poetry to "emerging writers." Our little cabal of three could do this presumably because we were "emerged writers." Anyway, sitting on a jury is often an eye-opening experience. There were the usual aesthetic disputes, the daydreamed throttling of one juror by another, the awarding of grants to people one wants to kill, and the occasional great moment of camaraderie. The food was pretty good too.

But the thing that struck me most was the nature of the manuscripts. Sometime over the past couple of decades, something really strange has happened to poetry in this country. And I wanna know why.

See, I did some statistical forensics of the two big boxes of submissions we had to go through in advance of our in-person meeting in Ottawa. I sorted the 89 manuscripts into categories. I called the first category "Projects" — these were book-length poems, or collections that were centred on a single project. Think Christian Bök's bombastic *Eunoia* or angela rawlings' elegant *Wide Slumber for Lepidopterists*. Think Herménégilde Chiasson's beautiful *Beatitudes* and Tom Walmsley's glorious *Honeymoon in Berlin*.

The second category I created was "Themes" — collections of poems all exploring a single theme or character. Like Paul Vermeersch's *The Fat*

Kid or Gary Barwin and derek beaulieu's *Frogments from the Frag Pool*. Adam Sol's *Jeremiah, Ohio*.

Next came what I called, for lack of something more succinct, "Themes in Sections" — either a book divided into, say, three or four sections, each exploring one theme, or a book containing several discrete projects. Alessandro Porco's highly entertaining *The Jill Kelly Poems* and Sharon Harris's *Avatar*. My own *Dead Cars in Managua* would just about fit into this file. Maybe Paul Dutton's *Aurealities*.

The final category I labelled "Miscellaneous" — collections of poems whose greatest connection is that they are all written by the same author. In other words, this latter category is simply a book of poems someone wrote. The best of what they had lying around, presumably.

Now, there are some good Project books, and some good Theme books, and some good books constructed as Themes in Sections. Great ones, even. But my favourite poetry books are of the Miscellaneous breed: an eclectic grab bag of poems by a single author. *Tulsa Kid*, by Ron Padgett. *The Nearness of the Way You Look Tonight*, by Charles North. *Primitive*, by Gil Adamson. I could go on.

In fact, I will go on, because you should read every goddamn one of these books. *The Bone Broker*, by Lillian Necakov. *Capitalism*, by Campbell McGrath. *A Defense of Poetry*, by Gabriel Gudding (okay, most of the poems in there invoke butts, asses, and rectums, but it's not truly a Theme book). *Rhymes of a Jerk*, by Larry Fagin. *Pearl*, by Lynn Crosbie. *The Romantic Dogs*, by Roberto Bolaño. *Flutter*, by Alice Burdick. *Shroud of the Gnome*, by James Tate. Jen Currin's *The Sleep of Four Cities*. *Your Name Here*, by John Ashbery.

Read them, you illiterate sods! Buy them and read them! (You'll never find a copy of *Rhymes of a Jerk*, but I'll make you a pirate edition for $75, okay?)

But I ask: Why so many stinking Project and Theme books? And why are writers who describe themselves as "emerging" writing so many of 'em? Shouldn't writers who are learning the art be trying out everything they can, creating a tangle of eclectic experiments, writing about any stupid thing that pops into their churning skull?

Where did this all start? It'd be easy — and fun, too! — to blame it all on Christian Bök, whose book-length poem *Eunoia* sold 14,000 copies and made a lot of young poets think they, too, could be superstars. Now, there's a book that you can describe to someone and make it sound interesting: "Oh yeah, so each section only uses one vowel! It's really cool. Yoko Ono! Umu Thurmun!"

But how do you make *Shroud of the Gnome* sound good? "There's all these poems and they're great and one of them's called 'Shut Up and Eat Your Toad'!" Just doesn't grab you in the same way.

I think, though, we can apportion the bulk of the blame three ways.

First, grant applications. Those "Project Description" requirements are evil fuckers, eating at the very fabric of our nation's poetry. Does a focused Project or Theme make for a better book of poetry? Nope — more often than not it means oatmeal-like homogeneity. Or some interesting idea stretched beyond its natural limit to achieve "book length." But it sure makes it easier to describe what you're working on when you have to fill out a grant application. Maybe it even makes the book you're applying for sound more important. Maybe it makes the writer *feel* more important.

Next, let's string up those goddamn MFA programs. Lucky for us, we don't have the kind of sausage-factory industry that's plaguing the U.S., but I think that's the hideous direction we're headed in. Again, it's easier to spend a couple of years working on something you can define in a concrete fashion, rather than something you can't — something more nebulous. Plus, again, a Project manuscript sounds *important*. It's more tangible: you can talk about it with your thesis advisor and it's like you actually have a topic for your discussion. I don't know that it's the way to write exciting poetry, though. So I hereby command all universities to shut down their MFA programs in creative writing.

Finally, there are the publishers. What the hell do they know? The "sales force" for their distributor has been whining to them: "We only have eight seconds to pitch a book to the buyers for Big Fucking Box Books. It's way better if we can say, 'A marvellous collection of poems about gardening and suicide' instead of 'Oh yeah, this is the new poetry book by L. Beau Noodles.'" A Project or Theme collection also makes it so much easier for publishers to write their catalogue copy. So there's all this pressure on writers to come up with poetry books that can be described as if they were novels.

This new concept thing with poetry collections — it makes me sad. It limits us. It makes art more convenient for marketing purposes. It's unkind to anarchy.

As for me, I really liked that snazzy hotel the Canada Council put us up in in Ottawa, but I'm throwing luxury behind and heading up into the mountains to start a guerrilla resistance. Join me. The food's pretty good. The cigarettes are filterless. ¡Venceremos!

July 2009

THOSE ARE PEOPLE WHO DIED, DIED

PEOPLE HAVE THIS powerful tendency to stop living, and then they don't exist anymore. I mean, to the extent that you can't sit around and discuss art with them or play pool or have tea with them. But you do everything you can to keep them existing in your head, or in your art.

And you are filled with remorse. You'd been meaning to call them, to take them for dinner, to let them know how much they meant to you.

This past winter, three fantastic artists — and friends, though none of them close friends — did the permanent exit shuffle. Each had made a great and unique impact on me, whether or not I ever got around to telling them.

The first to check out, on December 18, 2009, was Robin Wood. Robin was one of the great heroes in my life, probably my most profound influence beyond my parents. I first met Robin when I was about 20, going to York University for what would be a very undistinguished academic career, and my buddy Elliott Lefko, who went on to become a brilliant music promoter, dragged me into one of Robin's film lectures. I don't recall now what the film was, but it probably didn't matter: Robin's readings of films made almost any movie a rich, fascinating experience.

Enthralled, I wound up studying with him, including a course on Hitchcock and De Palma, as well as one each on Japanese and European cinema. Robin was fond of his students, and often invited us to parties at the downtown apartment he shared with his partner, the film critic Richard Lippe (with whom I shared an adoration of the magnificent Hollywood star Kim Novak).

I later became, for about ten issues, the typesetter and designer for *CineAction!*, the magazine of radical film theory that Robin co-founded with an eclectic bunch of exciting thinkers, including Richard, Florence Jacobowitz, Bruce LaBruce, Scott Forsythe, and Janine Marchessault. Through the courses I took with Robin, and my experiences with *CineAction!* and my friendship with Robin and Richard, I learned how to watch films, how to read them. I also learned how to read books. I learned a lot about writing and about thinking and about how stories are told.

I had never met anyone so radical and brilliant. Robin was a beautiful humanist. He was, I believe, the first English-language film thinker to take the French *auteur* theory seriously. His books on Hitchcock and Hawks are classics. Robin was 78 when he died. He had introduced me to my favourite film of all time: *Vertigo*. When he screened it for our class, he was choked up as he spoke afterwards, even though he had likely seen the film a dozen times or more. And he once dubbed *Texas Chain Saw Massacre* "the most distinguished American film of the 1970s," or something to that effect. You might find that claim laughable — until you learned what Robin saw in the film.

Just a couple of weeks later, I was saddened to hear that the artist and writer Barbara Caruso had died on December 30. Barbara had been married to the poet and publisher Nelson Ball for 44 years. She was sharp and lovely. Barbara was also a fascinating visual artist and the author of three important books: a collection of essays on painting and two volumes of journals from the 1960s and 1970s, all published by The Mercury Press. I don't know if there is a more honest and telling published account of an artist's life than the two detail-laden installments of *A Painter's Journey*.

Although not recently enough, I had visited a few times with Barbara and Nelson in Paris, Ontario, where they settled when they left Toronto. Barbara had always read my latest book and prepared challenging and absorbing questions, about my writing, or my life, or politics. And she talked with great precision about her own work: the paintings and drawings I got to see at a few gallery shows I made it to in Cambridge and Toronto, and the covers she had created for Nelson's legendary mimeographed Weed/Flower chapbooks. I learned so much in those few talks: apart from Brian Dedora, I'd never heard anyone speak so passionately — and clearly — about colour, about shape, about the field of the canvas.

We ate store-bought cookies, drank cup after cup of tea, and talked. Nelson offered few words, but clearly took great pleasure in watching Barbara engaged in the intellectual and the artistic. It always struck me that Barbara, in her visual art, and Nelson, in his writing, did such similar things: minimalist explorations of the most delicate subtleties, and of the canvas and page. They created with great care and deliberation, and with such commitment to their respective arts.

A few weeks into the new year, on January 21, 2010, there was a death we all knew was coming. Paul Quarrington, the writer and musician, who'd been diagnosed with stage 4 cancer the previous spring, took his leave. I'd planned to see Paul perform with his band, Porkbelly Futures, that weekend, but had received an email from a bandmate saying that Paul wouldn't be able to play, and that praying for him might be the thing to do.

I first met Paul in 1980, when he and I wrote three-day novels at This Ain't the Rosedale Library. Paul was a truly swell guy, and just in the early phase of his own writing career. Over the next three decades, I'd see him at various events — a Freehand Books launch, an Al Purdy tribute, a celebration of bookseller/publisher Nicky Drumbolis — and he always treated me like we were buddies. I can't even imagine the kind of warmth his *good* friends got!

In October, I skipped the big Harbourfront literary feting of Paul, going instead to a "solo" concert he was giving a few days later at Hugh's Room in Toronto's west end. Knowing that his time was limited, Paul had decided to perform every night he could, until he was no longer able. I brought my friend the poet Jim Smith, who had never met Paul. I worried that the night was going to be a dirge-like goodbye.

Jim and I arrived at Hugh's Room early, and Paul was having a drink in the foyer. As always, he was friendly and interested, and he treated Jim, too, like an old friend. Even with the clock ticking, he had time to meet someone new. The concert, as I later wrote Paul, was perhaps the greatest live-music experience of my life (better even than Randy Newman's 2006 concert at Convocation Hall, which Paul and I both attended). The night was pure celebration. An abundance of joy filled that room. Between beers, he sipped at a colourful health drink one of his bandmates was making for him. His old music partner Dan Hill joined him for a couple of songs, and Paul even played some new numbers: gospel-tinged pieces about his mortality. There was profound happiness in his face: I think he was blown away that he — probably best known for his funny songs — could write such glorious meditations.

Paul's example, in the last months of his life, was an incredible inspiration. He finished a book or two, cut a CD, and played scores of gigs across the country. A week or two after the show I saw, he began performing with an oxygen tank onstage. He wasn't going to let shortness of breath ruin his fun up there.

These three great people — Robin, Barbara, and Paul — they weren't people I saw often. I wish I'd spent more time with them. But I'm grateful for the time I did get with them.

Death got three of the really good ones. Hopefully no one else will die anymore.

July 2010

About a year after Robin's death, some friends got together and published his novel Trammel Up the Consequence *(do an online search: you can still order a copy). I'd seen a very early version of it a decade or two earlier. It was ambitious, brilliant, prickly, and difficult. I was so glad it was finally seeing the light of day.*

Paul, meanwhile, spent much of his allotted final year finishing his wonderful memoir Cigar Box Banjo *and his one and only solo CD, the beautiful and poignant and often funny* Songs, *some tracks from which he'd written when he knew his time was running out.*

And after Barbara was gone, Nelson and I became closer, maybe because he now had to do all the talking himself. I edited his first post-Barbara collection, In This Thin Rain, *for my Mansfield Press imprint. It was the first time Nelson had published a book without Barbara having read every poem first. I felt a great weight of responsibility, but it went very well. We did a second collection last year,* Some Mornings, *and have some more projects in the works. Although Nelson's poetry is going through some noticeable shifts, Barbara is still very present in his work. Perhaps more present than ever.*

A friend of Nelson's, Catherine Stevenson, has created a mesmerizing, essential video called Nelson Ball & Barbara Caruso / Home Project / A Photo Documentary. *Look for it online, and explore the amazing artistic partnership Nelson and Barbara shared.*

THIS IS MY FUCKING BOOK

HAVE I KNOCKED academia lately? It's hard to at the moment.

I'm in my office in Watson Hall, Queen's University, where I'm writer-in-residence this fall, thanks to the persistent efforts of Carolyn Smart, the no-bullshit poet and memoirist who does a brilliant job of running the school's modest creative writing program. Living in Kingston has been a transformative experience. In the past, I've organized readings, given workshops, mentored writers, and written. Here, I get to apply all I've learned at once. I'm meeting with students one-on-one in my office, organizing the Real Residential Reading Series in a campus pub, doing a night of Mansfield Press poets at another pub out in the community, leading a weekly slow-reading workshop, visiting classes and local writers' groups. And, as an afterthought, I'm getting a bit of writing done myself.

So I'm sitting there at my desk and in about 15 minutes I'm taking over a creative writing class while Carolyn is away. I see, by the miracle of the Internet, that Coach House Books has released a trailer for Gary Barwin's best book yet, *The Porcupinity of the Stars*. It's a big production: four minutes long, lots of funny imagery, locations all over downtown Toronto.

For some reason, it just bugs the shit of me. Not Gary's trailer itself —

the fact that now we have to make goddamn book trailers! It's not enough to write a book. To do launches and readings. To tweet and BlechBook. Now we have to be movie stars, too.

I have ten minutes before my class starts. I scrawl "Stuart Ross Book Trailer" on a piece of scrap paper. I open up PhotoBooth on my Mac and hold up my sign, wiggle it around a bit, put it down, and pick up my book. "Hi, I'm Stuart Ross and this is my fucking book. It's called *Buying Cigarettes for the Dog.* And it's got stories in it. And I hope you'll buy it." I grimace and fill the screen with my sign again, muttering. It's my first book trailer and it's 25 seconds long. I flip it in iMovie, turn it into a clip, then log into YouTube as farmergloomy, upload it, and share it on my BlechBook page and Twitter.

I look up at the clock. I've got a minute to get to class. In the class, I make a bunch of neat kids write a bunch of stuff. And when I get back to my office a couple hours later, 30 or 40 people have already watched my trailer.

Over the next few weeks, I do two more trailers. They are slightly more ambitious and increasingly awful. For the third one, I hum the *Batman* theme as soundtrack. Production values are where it's at. I do not compromise.

So it's going pretty good at the residency. See, the English department gave me a budget to play with. So I'm bringing in a lot of favourite writers — creating the dream readings I've always wanted to attend — and luckily the Grad Club venue is standing-room-packed every time: others are enjoying the readings too. David McFadden slays them. Lily Hoang produces delighted bafflement. Paul Dutton blows their lids off. Elyse Friedman makes them laugh. John Lavery casts a spell. Martha Baillie buries them in mystery. Rabindranath Maharaj charms them. Carolyn Smart commands them. And that's just half the readings.

Meanwhile, Queen's students and members of the Kingston community are coming in and out of my office. I love meeting these people and reading their work. Whether they are brilliant (as several are) or whether they are taking their first steps as writers (as many are).

I organize a reading for poets I've published through Mansfield Press. The Mansfield Poetry Invasion starts at five one Sunday at Ben's Pub and that afternoon there is a huge accident on the 401 just a few kilometres outside of town. Four of the six writers are stuck. They're texting me and phoning me. Luckily Jason Heroux lives here and Leigh Nash is already in town for a yoga retreat. Just as we begin, Jim Smith and Lillian Necakov arrive. We get a good crowd and I start playing for time — reading out text messages from stranded writers, lecturing on saddle stitching, telling jokes, photographing the audience, being an idiot. Great readings all around and, just as the last of who we have in the dugout gets up to present, Peter Norman finally arrives. Peter just spent four hours on the last 20 kilometres of the trip from Toronto. The audience is cheerfully entranced by the drama of the evening, and this night is getting mighty long. Peter delivers a trademark reading, and Natasha Nuhanovic shows up, exhausted. Soon she's up at the front of the big room, acing her 15 minutes.

A few weeks later, after a magnificent final reading by a dozen of the student writers, and writers from the community I worked with at Queen's, I find out from the Writers' Union listserv that my second book trailer — where I offer viewers the choice between a bent paper clip, an empty plastic Coke bottle, and my book — is on Huffington Post, where the question is asked: Is this trailer so bad it's good? Apparently not. At the moment it's voted 18th out of 19 book trailers. I cast my vote, giving it a one-out-of-ten rating. I am desperate to make last place!

Plus, I can't believe I'm on HuffPo, one of my favourite sites! Me and John McCain and Lindsay Lohan! A day ago, my trailer had about 140 hits on YouTube. After a few days on HuffPo, it's reached 3,200 hits. It's hovering around 14th. Last place is now just a distant dream. I am devastated.

It's amazing what you can accomplish when you put your mind and about ten minutes to it.

November 2010

I've made many more book trailers since (look for Farmergloomy on YouTube and you can see them), but none has achieved the sublime terribleness of that first masterpiece that changed the world. At 5,608 hits as of this writing, I'm giving Nicki Minaj a run for her money.

THE TERRORS OF TINY TOWN

OKAY, SO I lived in a big city for half a century, and then I moved to a small town about 75 minutes away. I didn't know what I was getting myself into. It took me leaving Toronto to realize why about half the membership of the Writers' Union of Canada lives in that city.

But it's not like I want to move back. Not entirely, anyway. When I left, so many of my writer friends were saying, "But I can't imagine the Toronto literary scene without you!" They seem to have adapted pretty quickly. My phone almost never rings here in Cobourg. And I don't get invited to give readings in Toronto anymore. When my name comes up on Queen Street West, they spit on the sidewalk and cross themselves.

So now I'm in this town of 17,000 people. There are a few writers' groups here, including the Cobourg Poetry Workshop. They have a reading once a month, at a place called Meet at 66 King Street East. So if you're going, you phone your friend and say, "Do you want to meet at Meet at 66 King Street East? Oh, it's located at 66 King Street East." Each reading there features one visiting writer and two local writers. It used to be that the workshop raised its funds by charging the local writers $25 to read with the visiting writer. This is among the weirdest things I've ever heard. But they don't do that anymore: you just pay $60 a year to be part of the cabal, which means you can go to their monthly workshop.

When I chose not to join — it wasn't the $60; just, I haven't belonged to a writing group since I was a teenager; it doesn't interest me — I realized I might look like a big-city snob or something. And maybe I do. When my name is mentioned here on King Street East, they spit on the sidewalk and cross themselves.

I moved to a small town because I thought it would be crazy to live my whole life in Toronto. I thought of moving to New Denver, B.C., population 600, a place I've visited every spring for the past five years. I love it there. But how the hell could I make a living? I considered Paris, Ontario, where Nelson Ball lives, and then I could visit Nelson Ball all the time and drive him crazy. But an opportunity arose (a woman was involved) to relocate to Cobourg. To a house just a three-minute walk from the lake. A space where I'd be able to have my own office. Rent is a lot cheaper in Cobourg, Ontario, than in Toronto.

And it sounded so fucking serene. There's a place here called the Buttermilk Café. Know what I mean? There's a store called Friendly Fires (they sell fireplaces, not ordnances to be used against your own troops): their slogan is "Fires That Are Friendly." There's a park with a bandshell, just like in a Mickey Rooney movie. Everyone owns a dog, and if you don't you get thrown into jail, which is now a bar called Al Capone's and the jail cells in the basement have cartoon crooks painted on the walls.

Goodbye, Toronto, and good riddance. Who needs the CN Tower anyway? I can see the bell tower of Victoria Hall from my study window.

Little did I know, though, that my literary career would plummet like a grand piano pushed off the CN Tower. I've got this novel out and it's barely getting reviews: some blogger wrote that it had no plot so she couldn't write a "synapsis" of it: it's just a big "mis-mash." When you leave Toronto, you are at the mercy of reviewers who write stuff like that and give you one star out of five.

I'm hungry for people to talk writing with here. I'm also hungry for Indian buffets. Friends come to visit, and they are charmed by this town. I beg them to move here. I offer to be their butler. "I could imagine living here," they say, and then they go back to Toronto and eat matar paneer for every meal and go to three literary readings a night.

So I experimented. I launched my novel, *Snowball, Dragonfly, Jew*, at a local coffee joint, the Human Bean. I was terrified no one would be there. But the place was packed out, standing-room only. Must've been 35 people. Some of them I didn't even know. One guy had a blog about Cobourg and he'd recently posted that I lived here and wasn't that just like learning that Tolstoy lived in your town? I thought his blog was a prank, but there he was at my launch.

I've learned that if you're in a small place and you want some culture, you have to create it yourself. So my experience at the Bean has encouraged me to start a reading series. I'll pass a hat to pay the writers who come. I'll promise them a tour of the old courthouse in Victoria Hall. They can look at the Friendly Fires sign. They can run around in circles on the bandshell and pretend they're Bon Jovi. I'm sure I can get a dozen people out to see them! Maybe 15!

Because otherwise I'm going to go crazy in Cobourg. Thing is, I like it here. But I'm going to go absolutely crazy. A million literary things are going on 75 minutes west of me in Toronto. (Tonight I missed a reading by David W. McFadden and Paul Vermeersch!) Half a million 90 minutes east of me in Kingston. (Tomorrow I might miss the book launch of my friend Sarah Tsiang!)

If I hadn't spent 50 years in the despised literary nexus of Canada, I probably wouldn't care. I wouldn't know what I was missing.

I would spend my time reading the zillion books I own and haven't read. I would write up a storm every day. Then go and contently watch the beautiful storm crackling across Lake Ontario, just three minutes away. I would get to know everyone in the Buttermilk Café by first name. I would meditate at the ecology garden. Take my sketchbook to Monk's Cove. I would be in heaven.

April 2011

Things change quickly in Tiny Town, I've learned. In the few short years since I wrote this, a splinter group broke away from the Cobourg Poetry Workshop to start their own group and series; Al Capone's turned into McAllister's and then got shut down; Friendly Fires changed their slogan; Sarah Tsiang and I are no longer friends; and though I've organized about half a dozen literary events here, I haven't started up a reading series yet. I sure do like walking my dog along the beach at midnight, though.

YOU, JOHN LAVERY, YOU WERE
AN INVENTOR

JOHN LAVERY TOLD the *Globe & Mail's* John Barber he'd never been happier. The author of two story collections and a novel, John had terminal cancer, was often in pain, rested rigorously for every public appearance, and faced a battery of chemo treatments and surgery. Six months later, at 10:22 a.m. on May 8, 2011, Canada lost its greatest literary acrobat; those of us who John knew well lost a great friend; and John's lovely family lost a John the rest of us barely knew. He was 61.

At the moment John said he'd never been happier, he didn't know how long he had left; he didn't want to know his "expiry date." In fact, he had a reading scheduled in Ottawa the day he died. A few months earlier, he and I read together in Toronto, his first and final reading in that city from his one novel, *Sandra Beck*. (If you're only going to get to write one novel in your lifetime, that's the novel you should write.) And a couple months before that, I had brought John to Kingston, where I was writer-in-residence at Queen's, to read in my Real Resident Reading Series. It was the final installment of the series, and I wanted John to be the culmination.

I suspect those readings took a lot out of John, as did the train rides from Ottawa (he lived in Gatineau), but he was in great spirits, and when he took the stage, he was no less than magnificent, flamboyant, masterful. He read in verbal and vocal flourishes, his hands sweeping through the air, pages of text drifting to the floor every minute or two. John took such immense pleasure in reading from *Sandra Beck*, the book he was determined to finish and see published (which then-Anansi editor Melanie Little made happen).

And at each reading, he embraced his guitar and sang the complex, unusual songs he was recording over that last year, the brilliant cascade of songs that would make up the CD *Dignity*, posthumously released at a celebration of John's life, writing, music, and artistic passions, on September 17, in Gatineau, a beautiful, rich, sad, happy event curated by John's remarkable wife, Claire Dionne.

I emceed the celebration with their daughter Madeleine, and read excerpts from John's story collection *You, Kwaznievski, You Piss Me Off* (has there ever been a better title for anything?); his other daughter, Catherine, read from one of John's favourites, French novelist Christian Bobin (John read almost exclusively in French); his son, Charles-Éric, performed a musical version of one of John's poems; and many other artists, friends, and relatives paid tribute through music and words. The afternoon ended with a video projection of John's reading in Toronto, pages of text drifting to the floor, and there was no holding back the tears then. Up there, on the screen, he was so viscerally alive.

If you haven't read *Sandra Beck*, you better. There is zero else like it in Canadian literature. I think John Lavery accomplished exactly what he wanted to. He was an inventor, the inventor of his own language, and his inventions were infinitely more exciting than the piles of samey-lite-hipness that get cranked out from Canadian presses every year.

I was once convinced I could write only out of depression. And when I visit high schools, I hear that a lot: *I can only write when I'm sad.* In fact,

I know a lot of adult writers who claim they can only write when they're drunk, hanging from a noose, or have their nose clamped in a vise.

I think depression, sadness, self-loathing, pain *can* trigger a desperate clawing for salvation through art. Of course, a lot of really bad art comes out of it, along with some good stuff. There is, perhaps, the sense that you can't write when you're happy. Or that anything you write is going to be crap about skipping through lush fields with animated bluebirds fluttering around your noggin. Or some nauseating thing about living the artist's life on Queen Street West and having huevos divorciados every morning with David Hockney, Miranda July, and a seven-foot-tall Imelda Marcos impersonator at Sand Between My Toast.

I don't know what state of mind John Lavery was in when he wrote *Sandra Beck* or the stories in *Kwaznievski* or his first book, *Very Good Butter*. But from the discussions I had with him about writing and about literature, and from reading his work, I think he might have been in a state of being in love with the possibilities of the language he wrote in. A state of euphoria over the possibilities, even.

Early that afternoon of May 8 last year, we received the last email from John's address, sent out by his daughters as per his instructions. It contained the text of his song "Disappearing." Here's the third verse:

> *I'm disappearing*
> *tell me can I get there from here?*
> *I'm ditching my high time,*
> *my single space, and my andro's fear*
> *and I'm moving on*

And here's the last:
Did you sleep well

The kitchen's closed,
I don't cook for bed lugs
Coffee?
It's cold. You'll have to
make some yourself.

I cried when I opened that email and realized what it signified. I had written to John a couple of weeks earlier and told him I wanted to come and visit him. He told me I'd better hurry up. I never did make that trip.

When I go to Ottawa, I miss John. In the Manx Pub, I gaze at the table we sat at when we first met, when I craned closer and closer to hear the soft rumble of his voice that nearly disappeared into our surroundings. In Ceylonta, I look at the table we always sat at, where he dug into his usual tandoori chicken, and I remember him telling me, when he was sick, that he'd never be eating that again. I really want that last conversation we never had.

I remember back to when John played at the 2010 ReLit Awards presentation at a pub in Ottawa. I had won the short fiction prize for *Buying Cigarettes for the Dog*. As always, when John performed, there was dignity in his voice and in his eyes and in his posture. There was respect for his own words. His long fingers prowled the frets of his guitar like a praying mantis. And he gave me a gift that evening that I value perhaps more than my ReLit ring. For me, John inserted a mention of Claude François into one of his songs.

I think he thought I was an idiot for loving the late French pop star, but he still gave me that. It made me happy.

December 2011

A PRICKLY (ON MY PART) CHAT WITH BRUCE KAUFFMAN ABOUT OPEN MICS AND OTHER STUFF

OVER THE FALL of 2010, I had the privilege of acting as writer-in-residence for the English department at Queen's University. Those few months in Kingston were pretty exciting — among the best periods of my life. I found a very welcoming community, got to know a lot of great people, helped to create some community, put on a heap of readings, ran some workshops, taught some classes, met with dozens of writers from the campus and community, drank a lot of beer at the Mansion, and attended local arts events.

One of the regular events I got to was an open mic at the Artel, a kind of artist-run, communal art space just off Princess Street, Kingston's main drag. The Artel open mic, which happens on the first Tuesday of every month, is the creation of Bruce Kauffman, who is as swell a guy as you can find anywhere. He also hosts a poetry show on Queen's campus radio station, CFRC. Bruce and I had several java meetings over the course of my stay in Kingston, and he came out to just about every reading I organized. So we saw a lot of each other.

But me, I have very little patience for open mics. Sometimes I want to run from the room screaming. How does one create a supportive test-ing ground for new writers and at the same time also encourage quality work? This question, which has plagued me for years as I've squirmed through the "I just wrote this poem on my napkin tonight" readings at the Art Bar in Toronto and elsewhere, needed to be answered.

So here, without further blah-blah, is my interview, via email, with my friend Bruce Kauffman, whom I just don't agree with.

ME: You've put a lot of energy into the Kingston literary scene the last couple of years, with your monthly open-mic series at the Artel and your weekly radio show on CFRC. You're supportive and enthusiastic, and you've channelled those qualities into cre-ating community and into providing opportunities for local writers to give their work exposure. Perhaps we can start with you explaining how and when each of those projects evolved.

BK: thanks for the opportunity and the kind words, stuart — my pleasure — and honoured to be a part of your project.

chronologically, the open mic poetry reading came first — so i'll start with that — a few years ago, my chapbook, *seed*, was published — and in the course of self-promoting over the peri-od of a couple of years or so, i moved next door to the artel (an artist collective) and thought that would be a perfect place for one of my readings, and then wanted to make it bigger than just me, so i included a 45-minute open mic ahead my own reading there in march of 2009 — the open mic was exciting that night and many came away pretty pumped and wanted to know when the next one was — so i canned the idea of me or any-one as a feature and launched the "poetry @ the artel" series in

may of 2009 as strictly three hours of open mic, and on a regular monthly night — there are reasons why i created it other
than the fact that there was a demand for it, but i'm guessing
that might be another question.

as for the radio show, after hosting the open mic for about
nine months or so, i was looking for a way to add another level,
or another dimension or something to it — i had indirectly
been involved with CFRC in a very limited way over.the
course of a few years but knew several volunteers who worked
there — so i was interested at the "listener" level and had indi-
cated an interest in becoming a volunteer myself — long story
short — i thought about the open mic series — i knew how
important that series was to all of those who participated, and i
thought of it as a way of taking their voices to a bigger audience and another level — if you think about it in those terms,
the title of the show, *finding a voice*, can really be interpreted or
read in a number of ways — after the initial idea was approved
by CFRC staff and a successful demo and shadow done, the
show was launched the first week of may 2010.

ME: Let's back up a bit now. What's the short-form version of your
background? When did you begin writing poetry? What writers
inspired you? And, finally, do you remember your own first
public reading?

BK: i'm originally from colorado — and began writing poetry in my
first-year university there — and although i continued to write,
i really didn't become passionate about it until about 1994 and i
believe it was in 1994 that i attended my first readings — and

it's somewhat of a chicken and an egg thing — not sure which came exactly first, but both the passion and the doing seemed to grow together — i religiously began to attend a weekly open mic/featured poet reading series for two or three years, then was asked to co-host and then host the series for about two or so years, basically until i moved to ontario in 1999 — and now i host both the monthly open mic poetry series and the weekly radio show here.

publishing history — research editor for the *poiesis poetry guide for colorado* (1998), several collaborations/anthologies both here and in the states, a chapbook, *seed*, published (2006), *streets*, a stand-alone poem published (2009), and a book review (*antigonish review* — john pigeau's *the nothing waltz* — 2010).

most inspired by w.s. merwin — far and away my favourite poet — but other poetic favourites have been/are whitman, william stafford, czeslaw milosz and pablo neruda — and as well rumi and gibran — but other than gibran and whitman, most of these didn't come into my life until the '90s — and, really, it was very early in my teens, probably the single author and event that most made me "understand" that i was a poet was the book (and as well the movie) *doctor zhivago* by boris pasternak.

i do remember my first public reading — at one of the weekly open mics mentioned earlier in this answer — so it would have been in the summer of 1994 — we each had four to five minutes and i was quite nervous.

ME: Like you, I also did a lot of early readings at open mics, mostly at the Axletree Coffeehouse readings in downtown Toronto. Unlike you, I find them pretty hard to take now (more on this later). You create a very warm and welcoming atmosphere at the Artel. What is your philosophy around open mics? What do you think they accomplish, for both those presenting their work and for the audience?

BK: most of my early readings, and my experience with open mics, were held in the daily grind coffeehouse in denver — and i guess my philosophy toward open mics might come a bit from those experiences — which i felt were also warm and welcoming.

and i guess, simply, the first tenet is that an open mic must be a place where any poet can come and feel "safe" — a place that encourages compassion, a place that feels inviting and encouraging — a place where anyone can come and not feel intimidated.

as for what open mics accomplish — i think there are as many answers as there are those who either attend or present — but i think it, in and of itself, inspires people — there is a bit of a kindred spirit there — i have seen it inspire people to pick up a pen after both short and long periods of neglect, to begin writing for the first time, to allow presenters to verbally share their words perhaps in a way that wouldn't be possible anywhere else, to get feedback, to pick up on a single idea or a seed that becomes something enormous and intense when they develop it into something else, and a fulfilled desire to touch others with a message presented in a deeply felt way — as for the audience, i feel their sense of accomplishment comes when they are touched or moved by another person's words.

but now i'm not guessing — personally, both either as a presenter or as an audience member, i go to poetry readings because in the doing i become more passionate about poetry in general and in my writing as well — and it was after my first reading that i truly came out of my shell — and kind of an aside here, to me, there really aren't very many things more beautiful than watching and hearing a poet read in front of a caring audience for the very first time.

ME: Okay, here's where I start to get lost with open mics. I do think it is important for people to be encouraged around their writing and made to feel safe in presenting it, but where does the quality of writing come in? What I see happen at open mics is that everyone gets wild applause. In fact, sometimes the most inexperienced writer gets the most applause. Is it possible that open mics reward bad writing much of the time?

BK: let's start this way — let's assume that there is importance to the quality of writing — especially in any eyes of the "editor," the self-editor, the publisher — couldn't the argument be as easily made that an open mic's reception and exposure actually create the space to allow the inexperienced writer to become "better"? — specifically, the environment allows and then encourages those inexperienced (and really any) writers to continue to write by "being around and hearing" other and diverse writers — put another way, the open mic space indirectly encourages more writing along with a possible exploration of depth, style, vision, and voice.

   now let's come at it from a different direction — "good" and "bad" — and let's deal specifically with poetry — what is a good poem anyway? — is it something that resonates — most probably — but nothing ever, anywhere resonates with everyone all the time — so does that, then, make any/every poem a bad poem — and then if it's okay that it's a good poem as long as a number of people resonate with it — where do you draw the line — what happens if only one other person resonates with it, or two — or ten in a group of 11 — or 100 in 60 million — the concepts of good and bad are obviously subjective in everything, but i feel definitely more so in art — i've long taken more of a taoist view when it comes to these terms in poetry.

for me — at an open mic and in each poem, i try to hear three things that really have nothing to do with quality — they are seed, voice, and heart — what "thing," in its own time, that touched the poet enough to pick up the pen at all, the sound it was heard in, and the place within that wishes to share the words and the message.

ME: Greeting cards and Harlequin romance novels resonate with tons of people too, but I don't think they're good literature. In response to your first point, though: if the aim is to encourage inexperienced writers to improve, wouldn't they do better reading some really good books of poems? As I said before, I think the consistently warm applause at an open mic encourages bad poetry.

But I'm getting the sense that you're not trying to create something that produces fine writing: you're more concerned with providing a safe forum for people to express themselves.

Do you think, though, that there is such a thing as a good poem and such a thing as a bad poem? I mean, aesthetic taste aside? Are you suggesting that quality is entirely subjective?

BK: i still feel that with anything written — it is ultimately about resonance — to start and simply for argument's sake — the fact that i, or you or someone else, might "think" that greeting cards and harlequin romances are not "good" literature is really quite irrelevant — moreover, the fact that we "think" — in itself, implies subjectivity — and if greeting cards or romance novels touch someone, move someone, encourage someone to read and to find joy in reading something, anything — i feel that is important — and looking at "good" from a different perspective — isn't that, in this way, "good" literature? and for them — we do not know where that goes, or what it leads to next.

   sure, the mission of the poetry series is to create an open, friendly and accepting space — and nothing else — it has never concerned itself with attempting to impress, but has felt that presence at times — i believe that "good" and "bad" as mentioned in the previous answer — are really just a simplification of what's in front of us — not just in poetry, but in all things — so i can't really go there — but, to try to explain these good/bad concepts i don't really believe in — this — does applause really encourage bad writing? to me that focus is too narrow — applause "can" do so many things in a broader sense — encourage confidence in the novice and the unsure, encourage commitment in the humble or the pragmatic, encourage capacity and growth in the sure and the involved — and that may lead nowhere, or down any number of almost infinite paths that i cannot, but someone may, predict and then deem as either good or bad.

   i shy away from the advocacy that there is an objective way to measure a poem — the "logic" behind that advocacy comes from the concept that 2+2=4 — but 3+1=4, 1+3=4, 47.27-43.27 also equals 4 — and what is 2 or 4, 2 apples does not equal 2 children crying — does not equal 2 suicide notes — does not equal 2 dead babies left in a dumpster … and even taking mathematics (perhaps the only objective thing i know — and even that is questionable) just a tiny step outside itself — it, too and immediately, becomes obviously subjective — so, by default, all other things, including quality, must be subjective as well.

ME: I don't think you're going to agree with my suggestion to lock open-mikers up in spartan rooms where they are forced to listen to recordings of Mark Strand and Alice Notley for days on end. (I believe this is called "poetry-boarding" — it may not be legal.) So let's move on!

Tell me about your anthology project with Hidden Brook Press. Do you see it as a new avenue, or something that has grown organically from the Artel event and the radio show?

BK: *That Not Forgotten* is the title of the upcoming poetry/short prose anthology with Hidden Brook Press and is set to launch late summer/early fall 2012. the call for submissions went out on May 1 and ran until October 31, 2011. the call was selective, only geographically — and even loosely at that. the only requirement was that the poet/author needed to have some connection, at some point in their life, to the north shore of Lake Ontario, in an area roughly from Kingston to Port Hope and north to the #7 Highway. the mission of the call, and now the book, is to paint "with an eclectic brush, reflections of, reaction to, hope within — pieces of ourselves found, pieces of ourselves lost here in this place."

there is both a wealth of talent and a generosity of heart here. there were over 100 poets or authors who contributed well over 300 individual pieces. as editor of the anthology, i am hoping to complete the second and final read/edit of the submissions by mid-December at the latest. following that, a determination of sequencing, order, possibly grouping and that type of thing — and then after that i turn it all over to Tai Grove, the publisher, and let him do his thing. we do currently have another call for submissions out, until January 31, 2012, for cover artwork for this anthology and are already getting a few submissions. the book, in the end, will be published by Hidden Brook Press/North Shore Series.

stuart, i can say that I have fallen in love with editing as much as i already had with writing and, yes, would love to pursue more of it. and i really believe all things are in process and equally interconnected, and i see perhaps editing and working on other projects as a growth both from and around the open mic poetry @ the artel reading series and *finding a voice* on CFRC — and that a growth from my desire to promote, encourage, and help nourish local talent — and that as well a growth from my love for the written and spoken word — and all of it flowing from the support of and the wonderful talent of others, and the genuine compassion found here in this city.

ME: Bruce, I really appreciate your time and patience with this interview. Clearly, you're a good guy and I'm a cynical asshole. But that's just how it is.

Bloggamooga, March 2012

I know I was right, I was totally right, everything I said, but how can you argue with a guy who says greeting cards are good literature because they resonate with some people? You just end up looking like a sociopath.

In fall 2014, I was driving home from Ottawa one Tuesday and realized it was Artel open-mic night. I figured it'd be nice to see Bruce, and maybe some old friends, so I pulled up to the venue just as things were about to get rolling. It was packed. Did I see all those terrible poets from a few years ago, having now improved because of the positive impact of the monthly open mic and all that encouraging applause and the excellent lessons they learned from listening to other lousy poets? No, none of those people seemed to be there. Maybe they were busy that night, or maybe they've given up poetry.

There was a bit of pain, but there were also some good writers. And I did see a few friends. I even signed up myself to read in the open mic — I had a bunch of new poems in my car I thought I might try out. I have to admit I enjoyed myself. And when they applauded — and I got a great reception — I appreciated the appreciation. Even though I was so quick to discount that same applause when it followed a crappy poet. Were things evolving? Were better writers starting to come to the Artel? Jeanette Lynes was there, and Eric Folsom, and Bob MacKenzie, whose poetry I'm not crazy about, read some decent fiction. I felt nostalgia for Kingston that evening. It was in Kingston that I became friends with the poet Jaime Forsythe, whose Sympathy Loophole, *which I published through my Mansfield Press imprint in 2011, is one of the best Canadian poetry debuts in recent memory. She's in Nova Scotia now. And I missed Nick Papaxanthos, whose own poetry debut I'll be putting out in fall 2015, and Christine Miscione, whose first novel I saw into print last fall. They've both also left Kingston. But the city is still full of exciting writers: Ashley-Elizabeth Best, Trevor Strong, Michael e. Casteels, Sadiqa de Meijer, Sarah Tsiang, Johnny Pigeau, and tons more, including famous people like Carolyn Smart, Armand Garnet Ruffo, Helen Humphries, Steven Heighton, Diane Schoemperlen, and Wayne Grady.*

*At the break, this young guy came up to me and raved about my writing —
he especially loved the humour (though I think, as I usually do, that most of what
I read was serious). I had planned to make a break for it at the break, hop in the
car, and head back to Cobourg, but this guy was going to read, so I stuck around.
He seemed like a smart guy. He was going to be good. I never did find out if he
was any good, because he got up there and started talking about his writing, and
bragging, and recounting his inspiration, and when five full minutes had passed
and he still hadn't read a word of his poetry, I shouldered my way out the door,
into my car, and onto Highway 401, where I'd be safe. Out of the radar of gentle, encouraging, all-embracing Bruce Kauffman, I could grind my teeth and hate
open mics again.*

THE PANDERINGOSITY OF
SPOKEN WORD

I GET SOME pretty good mail. Oh, wait, let me back up and put that into context. After all, I'm already so beloved in the spoken-word community, I have nothing to lose.

In a recent article in Calgary's *Fast Forward* weekly, the empress of Canadian spoken word, Sheri-D Wilson, declared spoken word the new small press. Actually, here's exactly what she was quoted as saying: "Our small presses are being diminished because of funding, and also because there's nowhere to sell the books, because independent bookstores are being crucified by the big-box chains. Spoken word is the small press voice in Canada. It is the alternative voice."

The idea that spoken word is the new small-press voice is absurd in more ways than I can express. As is the idea that small press is being diminished "because of funding" (what does that mean? because it's funded? or because funding is shrinking? *is* funding shrinking?) and because indie bookstores are falling like so many hideous rhymes at a slam.

I think Sheri-D doesn't understand what small press is. Because over the past month or so I have received a dozen exciting small-press items in my mailbox — most of them wouldn't even be carried by a bookstore. My friend debby florence, in Missoula, Montana, sent me a lovely handwritten chapbook that was part letter and part poem, created in an edition of one. "Dear Stuart" is now among my most treasured small-press items. Michael Mann in St. Paul, Minnesota, sent me a nice package, too: the latest issue of his long-running poetry magazine *Unarmed* and a chapbook by rob mclennan with graphics by the late Barbara Caruso.

And the other morning, I found a chapbook by Kingston poet Michael Casteels in my mailbox; he was in town and dropped it off. His poetry is getting better and better. And last week in Paris, Ontario, where we were launching my new book and the Mansfield spring poetry quartet, Kemeny Babineau gave me some beautiful chapbooks from his Laurel Reed Books — chapbooks clearly made with love. A few months earlier in the same town, when I was meeting Nelson Ball to discuss his Mansfield book, *In This Thin Rain*, he handed me a small, nifty chapbook from his tiny Rubblestone Press called *Nine Poems*: it contained the poems I'd edited out of his book.

Every week or two, small-press stuff winds up in my hands or my mailbox. I look forward to the erratic arrival of Larry Fagin's fantastic *Sal Mimeo* magazine. I used to get Benjamin Tripp's stapled mag *Gerry Mulligan* (now it's online, which I guess saves staples). From time to time I get big packages of broadsides and chapbooks from Greg Evason, who, like me, has been making small press for about 30 years.

Bookstores have nothing to do with small press at this level. This is a world that doesn't need bookstores, that barely knows what bookstores are.

Yeah, small press is Coach House and Anvil and Mansfield and Oolichan, and these publishers are struggling to find new ways to get their books out there with the diminishment of indie bookstores and the yoga-mat-ization of the big-box monsters. But small press is also the photocopied, mimeographed, rubber-stamped leaflets and chapbooks and scrolls that are cranked out by individuals in a world apart from bookstores or funding or universities. Small press is long poems and micropoems, short fiction and novellas, rants and manifestos, visual poems and flarf.

I'll tell you this: small press is those things, it is all those things, but it is not spoken word. Small press is about production, printing, publication. Design, typefaces, binding, paper stock. Tailoring the physical product to the written piece. How can spoken word be small press? Can pizza be baseball? Can iguanas be radio?

The other thing Wilson is quoted as saying is this: "[Spoken word] is fast. And it is socially relevant. It's about passion. It's not about saying things that you think people may want to hear."

But saying what people want to hear is *exactly* what spoken word is. Spoken word panders. It's about pleasing the audience, getting the most applause. Slams are popularity contests. They are entertainment. Lilt-o-thons.

Whereas small press challenges. Its very form and mode of creation can challenge the assumptions behind production and consumption in this capitalist society we're stuck in. And much of the best poetry published by small presses is difficult. It challenges intellectually and ideologically; it challenges the very idea of literature; it challenges through form or visual elements. It fucks with Shakespeare, it fucks with your Grade 8 English teacher, and then it fucks with you.

On a related note, in March, some stunned jury made Kris Demeanor the poet laureate of oily Calgary. There was a small uproar because Demeanor is a musician. He doesn't have a poetry book, or a poetry chapbook; he doesn't call himself a poet anywhere on his website. As of this writing, he doesn't even mention he's poet laureate on his website. He's a clever, entertaining singer-songwriter. A lot of poets saw his appointment as a stinging slap in poetry's face. Perhaps the jury wanted poetry to reach a bigger audience, make poetry more accessible. But naming a musician poet laureate is just bone-headed. Look at it from the other direction: I don't think Don Coles or Helen Guri or Alice Burdick or Louis Cabri are going to win Junos anytime soon (especially Louis Cabri).

Unlike spoken word, much great poetry isn't instantly accessible. Some of it has an audience of 17 people — not because it's bad, but because it's difficult, or esoteric, or experimental — and that's just fine. Trying to force poetry to be something that it isn't doesn't do poets or the art form any favours. Declaring spoken word the new small press is to not understand small press.

May 2012

The word bully *gets thrown around pretty readily these days. I got called a bully for writing this column. My old friend Peter Darbyshire, the fine fiction writer, ambushed me in the blog for the Vancouver* Province. *He invited Sheri-D to respond to my comments. She's clearly a nicer person than me because she told him she admired my work as a poet and performer. But then she said, "Ross's attack in* sub-Terrain *on me and the genre is bullying. ... It's what I call the conspiracy of silence. If you speak, it opens you up to more bullying. It forces you out of dialogue and into defence. Inevitably, it silences you and perpetuates fear. Dialogue is what we need in today's world because it gives voice back to people, where it belongs."*

That I was bullying or trying to silence was a surprise to me — what was actually happening was, in fact, that we were having a dialogue. I'm not interested in silencing anyone. And really, bullies are cowards: if I were a bully, I wouldn't be going after a strong woman like Sheri-D Wilson.

A year later, I got set up by another old friend of mine, and another fine novelist, Wayne Arthurson. In anticipation of the 2013 Edmonton Poetry Festival, he wrote a piece in Gigcity.ca about the controversy around the city's choosing a musician, Kris Demeanor, as poet laureate. Wayne knew I'd have a strong point of view about that. He called me up and interviewed me.

I told him: "If people can't tell the difference between a very good poet and a songwriter, they shouldn't be making decisions on who should be a poet laureate. … Clearly this so-called trend is an attempt to be populist, to try to popularize poetry by calling a rock star or a folksinger or a hip hop artist a poet. Well, here's the bulletin: poetry isn't easy. It's not a Big Mac and it's not a Green Day song."

Another friend, Vancouver poet Catherine Owen, was on my side and to the point: "[P]oets have few enough opportunities to take on public roles if they so choose. And it's called a poet laureate. Not a word laureate or a ditty laureate or a verse or doggerel laureate."

I didn't buy Demeanor's counterargument: "A lot of song lyrics are weak, as is lot of 'real poetry' by 'real poets' … The debate over what is poetry is less relevant than trying to be vigilant about quality, whatever the discipline."

Don't get me wrong. I like his music a lot. But to this day, his website makes no mention of him being a poet. Or having been Calgary's poet laureate.

Congratulations to Calgary for having a poet now as poet laureate — derek beaulieu. There's a guy who's vigilant about quality, and who identifies himself as a poet at every turn.

And a final note: I met an impressive young Toronto poet, fiction writer, spoken worder, zinester, and blogger named Whitney French last year. She didn't approve of my conflating spoken word and slam. She explained the difference to me. She made good points. I'm still digesting.

I LIVE TO SQUANDER

I'M NUDGING INTO my mid-50s, and wondering if I'll accomplish what I'd hoped to as a writer. But of course I won't. When I was in my 20s and publishing crazy poetry and fiction chapbooks, I wanted to have a psychological suspense novel published by Penguin Books before I was 30; that was my single concrete literary goal, arising from my obsession with the brilliant Patricia Highsmith. I missed that deadline. Not sure now if I have another few months or another few decades or another few minutes, but it probably doesn't matter. I won't be satisfied. I don't even *know* what would satisfy me.

One of my favourite poets when I was a kid was Stephen Crane, probably most famous for his tiny, eccentric, brilliant anti-war novel *The Red Badge of Courage*. One of his untitled poems almost describes my writerly psyche:

> *I saw a man pursuing the horizon;*
> *Round and round they sped.*
> *I was disturbed at this;*
> *I accosted the man.*
> *'It is futile,' I said,*
> *'You can never —'*

'You lie,' he cried,
And ran on.

I guess the difference between me and Crane's horizon-pursuer is that I keep running while *knowing* that I can never —

When I look back at my last 40 years (that's how long I've been writing and doing readings), I look at the choices I've made: doing so many things that don't directly contribute to there being books with my name on the cover. Things that are part of my writing life, but that get in the way of my actual writing.

Tonight I'll attend the Toronto launch party for the September 2012 issue of *This Magazine*, a publication I believe in deeply. I've stepped down as the Fiction & Poetry Editor, a position I held for a record-breaking eight years. I'd ushered through work by over 30 fiction writers and maybe 45 poets, some famous (David W. McFadden, Nelson Ball, M.A.C. Farrant), but more often new voices (Michelle Winters, Heather Hogan, Caroline Szpak). Famous or new, they all had to wait way too long to get paid and to receive their contributors' copies, but that's the story with a progressive political/cultural magazine run on a non-existent budget. I've passed my editorial reins on to poet/novelist Dani Couture: she was the only person I considered, and she said yes immediately. I left because I thought new blood would be good for the magazine, and because I wanted more time to do my own writing.

But I'm really going to miss the practice of curation — bringing exciting writing to an audience eager to discover something new. So in early August I clogged up all the new writing time I'd freed by starting up a new blog — The Week Shall Inherit The Verse: every week I put up a single fantastic poem by a different poet. The site is already getting a few hundred hits with each new work posted. Visiting theweekshallinherittheverse.blogspot.com means having to read only one poem; I think people like that, as long as the poem's killer. The blog does a lot toward satisfying the proselytizational part of me that used to inflict 300 Randy Newman songs on anyone who dared to drop by my apartment when I lived in the heart of Toronto.

That same curatorial urge got me involved with Denis De Klerck's Mansfield Press, where I've been acquiring books and seeing them through to print since 2007. It's thrilling to shepherd through books by people who've been my literary heroes for decades (McFadden again, George Bowering), and maybe even more thrilling to bring a writer's first book into the world (Jaime Forsythe, Robert Earl Stewart).

But once I get my Mansfield work out of the way, and I'm about to get down to my own writing, I realize it's Sunday night and I have to scramble together the Patchy Squirrel Lit-Serv. Patchy is a free weekly emailing that offers detailed listings about literary happenings in Toronto. I started it up almost six years ago (with Dani Couture, in fact), and Patchy now has nearly 1,000 subscribers. When I left Toronto for Cobourg a few years ago, I kept doing Patchy, even though I am increasingly estranged from Toronto's literary community and can rarely get to any of the hundreds of events I help promote.

There's been way more than this over the years — lit-related activities that are volunteer or practically volunteer. Like this column, for instance. The Meet the Presses collective devoted to promoting small-press literature. Editing weird little poetry magazines like *Mondo Hunkamooga, Syd & Shirley, Peter O'Toole, Hardscrabble*. Running reading series and organizing one-off events.

Very little of it, beyond my modest Mansfield honorarium, helps to pay the rent. I still have to do freelance editing, conduct workshops, and hold private writing-coaching sessions to cobble together a living. I mean, I love those things, too, but they get in the way of my writing. Sometimes it's hard not to feel resentful. But I'm making my own choices.

There are a lot of us who do this — organize, contribute, curate, blog, host — at the expense of our own writing. I think we probably all do it for the same reason: to bring into existence things we'd like to see exist. How many novels would Alana Wilcox have written if she hadn't taken over the editorial reins of Coach House Books? And what of Beth Follett of Pedlar Press? Brian Kaufman of Anvil Press? Bev Daurio of The Mercury Press and now Teksteditions?

Now, it might be that these activities help bring an audience to the things we do manage to write (while in elevators, on the bus, or waiting for the Bangles to come onstage at Casinorama and sing "Eternal Flame" 17 times). And somehow I do manage to squeeze out a book every year or three. (A great mentor of mine, the American poet Larry Fagin, who has taught hundreds of writers through the New School and privately, just launched his first trade book of poetry in about 35 years — the astonishing *Complete Fragments*, from Kyle Schlesinger's Cuneiform Press. Publication, you see, isn't the most important thing in the world.)

But like everything else around the subject of mortality, it's all about acceptance. I'm not going to reach the horizon I'm frantically pursuing. I'll never write that indefinable thing I'm striving to create. I'll just do my best, and enjoy the adventure, and try not to regret having squandered valuable writing time folding and stapling a couple hundred copies of a photocopied magazine called *Dwarf Puppets on Parade*.

September 2012

SHOAH, DON'T TELL

SO, COME A little closer, pull up a chair, and let me tell you a little story. This fucking maroon who once compared me to a Holocaust denier — because I was championing free speech — has on the front cover of his crappy new book of poetry this scintillating copy: "Humorous Verse." You know, just in case the reader isn't sure. Because it's always good to have instructions on how to respond to a book printed right there on the front cover. I guess the subtext is: "Even if you don't think this is funny, or didn't realize it was funny, please laugh because I meant it to be funny. I'm a funny poet even if you can't tell that I'm a funny poet."

I just looked up the etymology of my usage of the word *maroon* up there in the first sentence, and it turns out it's a mispronunciation by Bugs Bunny of *moron*. He's pretty funny, too, that Bugs. His whole carrot thing, his impossibly big front teeth. Munching away while cockily delivering that immortal line: "What's up, doc?" Though Bugs was officially born in Brooklyn in 1940, his earliest predecessor appeared two years earlier in an animated motion picture called *Porky's Hare Hunt*.

Let's take advantage of this fortuitous moment to examine the *Porky's* connection. In 1982, the live-action motion picture *Porky's* cemented a genre of film about teenage boys who occasionally saw bare breasts and regularly accidentally exposed themselves in public. *Porky's* was the biggest-grossing Canadian film of all time, outdoing even Christian Bök's *Eunoia*, which in turn outsold William Henry Drummond's *Habitant Poems*. The poster for Bob Clark's masterwork read: "Keep an eye out for the funniest movie about growing up ever made!" I remember being grateful for that poster — *Das Boot* had come out a year earlier and it was so long that you practically walked out of Cinema 1 from it and into *Porky's* in Cinema 4 the next year, so there was ample opportunity for getting your emotions all confused. "*Das Boot* mopey; *Porky's* funny" was our mantra in those days.

Anyway, here's the point: I have ordered a recall of all Canadian poetry books so they can be properly labelled. Rhea Tregebov's "Sombre Verse," Clint Burnham's "Incomprehensible Verse," David McGimpsey's "Witty But With Sad Moments Verse," Karen Solie's "Tractor Verse," Michael Lista's "Pompous Verse," and so on. If you're wondering how I have the power to have these authors' books recalled, don't forget my first-ever Hunkamooga column: "I Am the King of Poetry." And it's true: even though I'm not listed in *The Canadian Encyclopedia* like Kevin Connolly and Margaret Christakos and Jeramy Dodds (who only has one book published and it sold fewer copies than *Habitant Poems*), I am in fact the King of Poetry.

Wait, no! I am reversing that poetry-book recall! I just remembered: "Show, don't tell." You've likely never heard that advice, so I'm regally sharing it with you. If you can actually make your art evoke the thing you want to evoke, it's better than just saying: "This is a bunny going bowling." Besides, if someone wants to find Tregebov funny or Burnham comprehensible, that's — as Shania Twain would say, and I bet she has an entry in *The Canadian Encyclopedia* — their prerogative.

It's a free-speech thing, how people choose to respond to poetry. So that makes people who read poetry Holocaust deniers.

Which reminds me: when I was writer-in-residence at Queen's University, I met a great prof named Laura Murray. Visiting her class, I knew immediately she was a creative, engaging educator (even if she's on the wrong side of the copyright-licensing debate). Anyway, a few weeks ago, she invited me back to Kingston to talk with a class of about 200 students. She had put my novel, *Snowball, Dragonfly, Jew*, on the curriculum. It's about a guy (pretty much me) whose mother (pretty much my mother) may have assassinated a Holocaust-denying neo-Nazi (pretty much — Oh, wait, I changed his name just before the book went to press so as not to glorify the prick).

After I read a bit from the novel, and talked about the crazy process of writing it — this tiny novel that took me eight years to complete — Laura opened the floor to questions. After the usual gap of silence punctuated by chair-scrapes, hands began to go tentatively up. One student said, "The protagonist seems to be struggling with an identity crisis, but there's a chapter near the end where he lists all these musicians and writers and artists who have influenced him. Are these actually artists who have influenced *you?*"

"Yeah," I said, "that's pretty much my list and my crisis."

"Well, there's no identity crisis then: the character is defined through all those lists."

I had never thought of that. My identity crisis was cured.

Another student said, "On the novel's cover, there are the pages of a book that are torn up and shuffled out of order. Is that supposed to reflect how the chapters inside are all shuffled and out of chronological order?"

I looked at her in disbelief: disbelief, because I had never made the connection.

It really is the best thing when you visit a class and you learn about your own writing. And if it's a paid class visit, then you're actually getting *paid* to learn about your writing.

After the class ended, a few students stuck around to talk. The last one in line said, "I was struck by the circumcision imagery in your novel."

"Circumcision imagery?" I said.

She grinned, because it was so obvious: "When the Nazi gets shot, his hard hat flies off his head and hovers in the air. The hard hat is like the head of a penis, so it's like the foreskin gets shot off the guy."

I couldn't argue. How could I not have seen that?

And then she delivered the clincher: "So when he gets assassinated, the Nazi is made into a Jew."

Incidentally, *Snowball, Dragonfly, Jew* recently co-won the Mona Elaine Adilman Award for Fiction & Poetry on a Jewish Theme, given out by the J. I. Segal Committee of the Montreal Jewish Library. It was pretty exciting to be recognized, finally, as a Jewish writer. I don't win a lot of awards, but it's nice to end this on a positive note.

And, by the way: it's not like I'm bitter, but fuck *The Canadian Encyclopedia*.

December 2012

A DESPERATE, CHILLING RACE
AGAINST TIME

THIS BOOK YOU'RE holding right now? I'm editing it at this very moment. Revising old columns, adding in some follow-up material. And now writing a new essay to tack on to the end.

See, I haven't yet told Brian, my publisher at Anvil, but I'm actually going to release two books in spring 2015. He thinks I'm just doing this book. But all that changed about 18 hours ago, when Jason Camlot, who runs the Punchy Poetry imprint at DC Books in Montreal, sent me a note and asked me if I had a poetry book ready to go for this coming spring. Presumably the book he had scheduled got delayed for some reason, or else the author pulled it at the last minute, and Jason tried 15 or 20 other poets before he tried me. But I received a big grant from the Ontario Arts Council to write a heap of weird-ass poems and I was happy to get those weird-ass poems into the world. A working title I'd been kicking around for a few years, *A Hamburger in a Gallery*, was going to be a reality.

Well, I'm 55 years old right now. I'm working on 13 different book projects. If only one of those appeared each year, I'd be 68 before I caught up. But I wouldn't catch up, because what I do is I constantly add new book projects so that I can avoid finishing the other ones. But what's happened now is that it's a race against time. I want to finish these projects and I want to see them in print.

Come to think of it, I have *three* books launching this spring. The third is a co-translation, with Michelle Winters, of Montreal poet Marie-Ève Comtois' second collection. The English title is *My Planet of Kites*. It was supposed to come out last fall, through Mansfield Press, but I delayed it a season because there was a lot more work to do before I could feel confident about it.

Used to be I would knock rob mclennan because he is only eight years old and he has published 47 books. Whoops — another one got published as I was writing that sentence! Now he's published 48 books. (I'm trying to be nicer to rob these days, because a) I'm becoming an old man, b) rob married someone I like, and c) rob's done some pretty good stuff for other writers and that should be recognized.) And then there's George Bowering, who has published 104 or 105 books as of this moment; George turns 80 next year. Well, I've never published more than one book in a year, but that's going to change now.

Here's what I'm working on at the moment: three novels, one of which is a kind of sequel to *Snowball, Dragonfly, Jew*; this here book, *Further Confessions of a Small Press Racketeer*, the follow-up to my Nobel Prize–winning *Confessions of a Small Press Racketeer* (can you win a second Nobel?); a memoir of my life up until my mid-30s; a book of short stories with several appearances by Claude François; three collaborative poetry books — a long poem with Jaime Forsythe, a sonnet collection with Richard Huttel and another collection with Michael Dennis; three solo poetry books, including the one I'm going to do with Jason's imprint this spring; and the Marie-Ève Comtois co-translation.

I just spoke with Gary Barwin on the phone this morning, to determine whether or not I was crazy for taking on a second book in a single season. When I accepted Gary's wondrous poetry collection *Moon Baboon Canoe* for my Mansfield Press imprint last year, I made sure he didn't have another book coming out the season immediately before or after. And now here I was, going all Bowering-mclennan. Gary questioned whether the small-press world needs to emulate the big presses when it comes to this stuff. "I'll buy both your books next spring," he said. He also questioned what difference it might end up making in book sales. We're talking about such low numbers to begin with. One of the books might sell 20 or 30 copies fewer than it might otherwise have sold? And before the conversation was over, we agreed to write a sequel this year to our collaborative 1995 novel, *The Mud Game.*

When I was mulling this over last night, I thought about my declining presence in Toronto. I moved to Cobourg four years ago, and I'm no longer the mover-and-wobbler I was in the Toronto literary world. It's not that people have necessarily forgotten about me, but that a new generation of writers has begun to flourish, and an old geezer like me is not on their radar. So I thought: what if I attempted recognition through critical mass? This past year I have set a few personal records: I've had three chapbooks out — from Michael Casteels' Puddles of Sky Press in Kingston, Linda Crosfield's Nose in Book Publishing in Ootischenia, and Jay and Hazel MillAr's BookThug in Toronto. And for the first time in decades, I made a big push with mag submissions, and as a result, poems of mine have recently appeared in *Jubilat, Fell Swoop* and *Gargoyle* in the U.S.; *Event, Cosmonauts Avenue, Matrix, Stone the Crows!* and *illiterature* in Canada; and *Cordite* in Australia.

Beyond that: there is Donkey Lopez, the improvisational sound trio of which I am a member, along with musical geniuses Ray Dillard and Steve Lederman. We put out our first CD last spring, *Juan Lonely Night,* and we're planning on releasing one more — *Working Class Burro* — early in the New Year. And in spring 2016, I have another poetry collection lined up for release. It has a sort of religious title: I want this book, like *A Hamburger in a Gallery*, to be different from anything I've done before. Perhaps there'll be another chapbook or two before then.

So maybe all this activity will mean something. Maybe it'll stir up some interest in my work. Maybe I'll finally get another writer-in-residency. One thing is for sure: I'm this much closer to not having to think, as I get run over by a bus tomorrow, "Fuck, I'll never finish those 13 books now!"

If the bus holds off long enough, maybe I'll actually catch up to the horizon.

January 2015

MICHAEL DENNIS: THE NICE-GUY SIDE OF A NASTY PRICK

I'VE KNOWN OTTAWA poet Michael Dennis since the early 1980s. We met in Toronto when I was selling my chapbooks out on Yonge Street and he stopped to buy one. We became fast friends, though I found him sort of intimidating. Still do at times. But, in spite of a few rough patches, it's been a great and enduring friendship.

Michael is the author of over a dozen poetry books. Among my favourites are *Coming Ashore on Fire* (Burnt Wine Press, 2009), *Fade to Blue* (Pulp Press, 1988), *Sometimes Passion, Sometimes Pain* (Ordinary Press, 1982). In early 2013 Michael started a new project: he decided he'd blog every two days about a poetry book he likes. He is one of the most well-read poets I know, so this seemed a natural for him. Except that it involved a computer and the internet, and he is a Flintstone.

But he's done an amazing job with Today's Book of Poetry, and has already made a great contribution to the art and industry of Canadian poetry, and poetry from afar. Every day, this secret weapon in Canadian poetry becomes less secret. In December 2013, I interviewed Michael by email.

ME: Michael, since February or March 2013, you have been writing about a different book of poetry on your blog every two days, more or less. Are you crazy?

MD: No, not crazy, but you could say I've rediscovered my enthusiasm for poetry. As it happens, I have lots of time on my hands; I spend two or three hours a day on the blog. Thankfully I have a very supportive partner who sees that this project is important to me.

ME: How did you come up with the idea for Today's Book of Poetry?

MD: I had been writing little blurbs on Facebook from time to time to mention books I'd enjoyed, and they were primarily poetry. My friend Christian McPherson suggested I start a blog. Initially I had no interest. Then he said that if I blogged about poetry, publishers might send me books. That was the real hook.

I have been collecting poetry since I was a teenager and the idea of getting books in the mail was tremendously appealing to me. But I was very skeptical.

Christian actually set up the blog for me; there is no way I could have or would have, and I started with books I owned. Within two weeks I had a couple of different publishers sending me books. I was astounded. Kitty Lewis at Brick Books and Hazel Millar at BookThug were both big supporters right from the start. In fact, the encouragement of people like Kitty and Hazel really made the blog far more real for me. Once I started to get books from publishers, I quit writing about any books that didn't come from a publisher. It's one of my rules now.

ME: One of your other rules is that you write only about books you like. I know we've discussed this before: what's your rationale, and how much do you have to like a book? Is "good enough" the criteria, or does it have to be great, or excellent?

MD: Excellent is best, but I guess the criteria is whether or not I like it enough that I would suggest one of my friends read it. I've always felt that finding one really good poem in a collection made that collection worthwhile, but I'm certainly not using that criteria here. All the books I've chosen to write about are books I would happily put into the arms of a friend. Certainly some are stronger than others — but all of them contain enough of one thing or another that I was entertained, challenged or interested at some committed level.

I'm very naive sometimes and was surprised to find myself feeling terribly guilty every time I passed on a book, for whatever reason. I felt a real obligation to the publishers who were sending me books, that I should write about each of them, but as you said, I only write about books I like, books I like well enough to recommend.

ME: I don't think you should feel guilty! But how come you don't write about why you don't like a book? You're coming off as too nice a guy!

MD: Stuart, you know me so much better than that. I did think about the reasons I only wanted to write about things I like. One of them is my "tool set." As much as I love poetry and have a degree in English literature, I don't feel I have the skill set to deconstruct other people's poems. I would call what I do "appreciations" more than reviews — but I'm not out to break new ground. There are critical reviewers out there who do a fine job of deconstructing poems, but I never sought to do that.

But that really isn't it. I'm a nasty prick as often as not and full of vitriol to the brim — that doesn't mean that is the person I want to be. I figured I would write about the positive, and if I didn't feel the positive, I wouldn't write at all. There is only so much time and I didn't/don't want to spend my time exploring things I don't like, don't enjoy, don't approve of. To put it another way: I didn't want to spend my time talking about burnt toast.

The blog and everything associated with it is entirely my responsibility — so I get to set the parameters. If people and publishers don't like it, I guess I won't be doing it for all that long. But as it stands, as long as publishers will send me books, I'll be blogging about the ones I like.

The other side of that coin is the joy I mentioned earlier. I'd gone through, for a variety of personal and professional reasons, a period where some of the shine had come off of poetry. I felt terribly discouraged and frustrated and was withdrawing from my involvement with poetry. When books started coming through the door, I was astounded by a couple of things right from the start. The first of them was that I didn't know what I thought I did.

For the best part of 40 years I have called myself a poet and acted accordingly. I've been reading all I could and collecting all I could afford. I felt confident I had a good grasp of the poetry scene in Canada. I have never been more wrong. The flood of poetry that came to my door was a joy in itself; the surprise was the number of authors I'd never heard of. How could that be? Literally hundreds of books of poetry published in the last couple of years and a vast number of them by poets I'd never heard of. Once I got over my initial embarrassment and shock, it was an uplifting discovery. The best part of that was/is the quality. Of course there have been books I didn't like, but they are a minority. So many of these books are so good it makes me laugh, real happy laughter.

And it made me feel better about my own life as a poet. A great deal of the frustration I'd been feeling about my own work — and the lack of attention it received — evaporated. I honestly felt a rejuvenating glee at seeing these fine books.

With all of these books to write about, and I am trying to keep to one every two days (surgery and subsequent recovery have caused some gaps), I choose to not have the time for those books I would only criticize.

ME: What effect has this rigorous practice of writing about a book every two days had on your own poetry?

MD: I've always been a writer who wrote something almost constantly. I've been keeping a journal since I was a teenager. Over the years I've had many periods when I wrote less for one reason or another, and I was certainly in one of those periods when I started the blog. I continue to write poems but haven't been nearly as active in recent months. But this is one fallow period where I'm enjoying the break and certainly feel like I am fuelling up. This is a real learning process for me. I've always

131

read a lot of poetry, at least a couple of books a week, but since I started this blog I'm probably reading six or seven or eight books of poetry every week.

But to get back to the question, I am still writing. I have a chapbook coming out sometime this fall with Warren Dean Fulton's Pooka Press in Vancouver, *Blue Movies for Blues Players or Sonnets for the Eternally Sad*. These poems are about gender and power in film, believe it or not. I originally wrote them for a film course I took at Carleton University. The professor, José Sanchez, was a revelation, and the course a genuinely eye-opening experience. I liked these poems a lot and shopped them around a little. Warren very kindly agreed to publish them and I'm thrilled. I continue to write other poetry, but it isn't a priority at the moment. Frankly, I'm getting my poetry fix with the blog.

ME: Some of the books you've written about have surprised me: some pretty experimental stuff. Is this process of doing the blog broadening your aesthetic?

MD: I hope so. I follow the same procedure with each book. I try not to read anything else about the book in question so I don't have any preconceived ideas about it. When I'm reading these books I keep pen and paper handy and make notes; I jot down the poems that I find striking and proceed from there. With the more experimental works that you are talking about it was simple really — as I was reading and making notes, it was clear to me that these books had marvels in them that I was just beginning to understand, or appreciate.

132

It's not like I've had a change of heart or direction, I'm still partial to narrative poetry; I like a good story and a little dirt under the fingernails. But certainly there is an attempt, by me, to have a broader window to look out of.

Perhaps it's this: every time I open a book, I really *want* to like it. I want to find the joy someone felt with each and every book when they decided to publish it. Of course, that isn't always the case. Some books mystify me. I cannot begin to imagine how more than one person admired the poems. Those are the ones I don't write about.

ME: What is the fate of those mystifying books? Your bookshelves are already pretty crammed!

MD: Those books, the ones I don't blog about, end up on my shelf in alphabetical order, just like the rest of them. It's never been a criterion of mine that I had to love every book on my shelf. There are certainly some Irving Layton books I care for more than others — but that doesn't mean I don't keep them all. And I can always build more bookshelves.

It's not that I'm a completist, but I am a collector of sorts. You've been to our home and seen the art K and I have collected over the years; it is a bit of the same thing. You don't have to love everything equally to appreciate it, or keep it, as long as you recognize it has value to you. And of course I'm not talking about monetary value — emotional currency is more like it.

ME: What you're doing is important. There is less and less space for poetry to be reviewed in this country, so intelligent, enthusiastic bloggers are key to getting the word out about books from small presses. But how do you get the word out about your blog? How do you let publishers know you exist? And any idea how many people are reading your appreciations?

MD: The number of readers so far is almost 20,000, and I guess that works out to around 100 a day. When I first started the blog I had emailed or otherwise contacted a long list of Canadian publishers and explained what I was doing. Since then I have broadened the list to include a couple of American presses. I figure I've contacted about 150 different small presses and had responses in the form of books from 42 of them.

As I'm a total Luddite, I really am at a loss as to how to get a better readership. When I publish a blog, I contact the press/publisher in question and send them a link to the blog. If it is possible, I post my blog on their Facebook homepage. I also try to contact the author and send him or her a copy of the blog. Otherwise I post it on Facebook. I figure most of the people who read the blog are doing name searches for the writer and they get directed to the blog, but in truth I'm not sure how it happens.

I appreciate that some people find this important, the blog about small press poetry, and I think it's important as well. Not that what I say has particular importance or relevance, but that there is another voice championing these books. There really is a wide, wide universe of small press poetry in this country that so many readers don't know about, and it's not their fault. If *I* didn't know how broad it was — how many presses there were, how many great books — it would be hard for people outside the poetry world to know either.

One of the ways I can gauge the success of the blog will be whether those presses who've sent me work will continue to send work as time goes on. Of course I want to please readers, but I also want the publishers who are sending me this work, at considerable expense, to feel they are being treated with respect and courtesy.

And that leads me to talk about how I choose which book I'll write about. It's simple. I write down each book/publisher/ author when it arrives and write about them in first-come, first-served order, one publisher at a time. If I don't like a book enough to blog about it, I try to choose another from the same publisher so they don't lose their place in line. If I don't have another book by that publisher, I move on to the next.

As for letting more publishers know I exist, that's next. I've posted 113 blogs in a little less than eight months. The next time I send an email to a group of publishers, I'll have that as ammunition. Right now I'm waiting to see what will happen with all the fall releases and crossing my fingers.

ME: What's the future of Today's Book of Poetry?

MD: For the foreseeable future, it will be staying the course. I'm pleased with the response thus far. I'm enjoying the process far more than I ever thought possible. So the easy answer is that as long as books keep coming, I will continue to blog. I'd like to learn a little more about the tech side of things so I could add more additional information, pictures, links and such, but that will come. I'm a slow learner.

I'm glad there are people out there who see this blog as an

important addition to the world of small press poetry. It allows me to be involved in the conversation in some small way that I could never have predicted.

ME: Can we expect a review of Michael Dennis's next book on Michael Dennis's poetry blog?

MD: No, I don't think I'll be reviewing my own book. Besides, I'm not sure I could wax eloquently enough about its virtues.

Bloggamooga, October 2013

Postscript: As of this writing, Michael has written about more than 300 books and his blog is averaging 200 hits a day. He's had 85,000 readers in total from 121 countries. Check him out at michaeldennispoet.blogspot.ca. I still wish he'd write some negative or mixed reviews. But it's his blog, not mine. Oh, and his chapbook from Pooka Press never happened. Any chapbook publishers out there interested?

CRAD AND I

THE RECENT NEWS that the author of *Terminal Ward* is terminally ill has saddened me immensely, and it's given rise to a lot of conflicting impulses. While I've known Crad Kilodney for nearly 35 years, it's been a decade or so since he and I have exchanged more than a cursory email.

When I met Crad, I was in my late teens and I lived in Toronto. My friend Mark Laba and I were doing a lot of two-voice sound poetry readings. We were kicking around the idea of doing public guerrilla readings, such as on the escalator of the Eaton Centre, or out on city sidewalks. It was 1978 or 1979. Downtown, one day, I came across Crad selling his books on Yonge Street. He was flogging his first chapbook, *Mental Cases*. I bought it, of course (as I bought every book that Crad ever published), and was inspired by this idea of standing out on the street with a stupid sign around one's neck, selling literature. I got to know Crad a bit, learned how he'd made his chapbooks, where he got them printed, and so on. I soon started working at York University's student newspaper, *Excalibur*, and had access to typesetting equipment (this was before the days of personal computers, and long before the era of desktop publishing), and I decided to follow in Crad's footsteps.

Before then, I had made two publications, *Africa: A Tale of Moscow*, a small mimeographed collaborative story with Mark, and *He Counted His Fingers, He Counted His Toes*, a 12-page unstapled photocopied chapbook containing about eight poems. But now I was going to publish in quantity, and get my work printed professionally, like Crad's. My first book was *Bad Glamour*, in an edition of 1,000 (again, following Crad's example). It contained mostly poems, and a few very tiny stories. Crad encouraged me all along the way. In fact, in the early days, he and I often sold our works in neighbouring doorways on Yonge Street. Which was ridiculous from a commerce point of view. Anyway, if I hadn't met Crad, I likely never would have sold my work on the streets, though I certainly would have continued self-publishing.

For my second chapbook, I couldn't come up with a title. I was at Crad's place in North York, where we were eating some fried chicken for lunch, the football game on in the background as always on these Sundays. Crad asked to see what would be in the chapbook. Within about a minute he had zeroed in on a line in one of my poems. "This is the title right here," he said. "*When Electrical Sockets Walked Like Men*." And that was the title I went with. That was a pretty influential moment for me: I have, ever since then, had a fondness for long and stupid titles. Anyway, out on the streets, I wound up selling about 7,000 chapbooks over the course of a decade. I think Crad sold about 35,000 during his much longer street career.

Book titles and entrepreneurship aside, I don't think Crad was a significant literary influence on me. I was reading a lot of insane fiction back then: Bill Hutton's *The Strange Odyssey of Howard Pow*, Spencer Holst's *The Language of Cats*, David Young's *Agent Provocateur*, stuff by Opal Louis Nations, Donald Barthelme, William Kotzwinkle...and Crad. These were the kinds of things I liked to read and the kinds of things I wanted to write. But Crad certainly influenced me in the DIY spirit: this was shortly after punk had begun to break in North America, and I was very excited by bands like the Clash, the Sex Pistols, the Talking Heads — and various local Toronto punk bands, like Martha & the Muffins, the Wives, (formerly the Battered Wives, I'm afraid), Crancky Tom (led by the effervescent Liz Dixon, a friend who died way too young in 2007), and Blibber and the Rat Crushers, who were putting out their own cassettes and vinyl.

And although I'd published a couple of very small-print-run chapbooks, Crad inspired me to get out there and actually get in people's faces with my books: confront them with my weird poems and stories right on the street. It's possible, too, that Crad taught me to not compromise, and not to pander, in my writing. I'll give him that, as well. I get the feeling that if I keep on thinking about it, I'll come up with even more ways Crad influenced my thinking.

In the broader view, Crad Kilodney, so far as I can tell, has had very little influence on literary Canada. I suspect he is a pariah in academic circles, and certainly commercial circles, and those are powers that determine littaste. But through his street-selling, and through the hand-selling of Crad's books by Charlie Huisken, Gord Ames, and Dan Design at This Ain't the Rosedale Library, Crad inspired a lot of young people who were disgruntled about CanLit and had no interest in Alice Munro, Michael Ondaatje, and the other superstars. He encouraged a few other writers to self-publish and stand in the streets, including Arno Wolf Jr. (pen name for Timothy Weatherill), Lillian Necakov, Michael Boyce, Mark Laba, and me. He encouraged people involved in DIY — whether they were making books, or zines, or music cassettes.

He is and always has been a fan of the transgressive and of independent thought. A fan of kicking against the establishment. Crad was a fan of neo-Nazi Ernst Zundel, who published absolutely bonkers books laced with anti-Semitism and conspiracy theory — Crad championed free speech to a radical extent. He once led a group of us in a sit-in at the office of Ontario film censor Mary Brown, where he argued eloquently against censorship of movies in our province.

There was other activism, too. I remember typing up a copy of a long, dry story by Luigi Pirandello, one of about a dozen stories by renowned writers submitted to CBC's story contest in a hoax brilliantly orchestrated by Crad. I also remember joining him in an application to the City of Toronto to hold a book-burning at the intersection of Yonge and Bloor. He felt that Toronto was so anti-intellectual that it might as well embrace one of the practices of another anti-intellectual culture that once burned books. (We were told by the City that only food could be barbecued on the street, and were denied a permit.)

I spent a lot of Sundays at Crad's place, playing chess. Crad was a mediocre chessplayer, and better than me. We played a lot of chess; and he had the football game on TV (I could care less); and he'd show me crazy literature he'd been collecting — documents from religious cults and marginal political organizations, porn mags with three-breasted women, and more. Like me, Crad read some chess books, learned a lot about the masters (most of whom were bat-shit crazy, so that was fun), and never became a good player, so far as I know. I still play an awful lot, mostly online. I'd like to play Crad again, and see where his game is at.

Lorette Luzajic, a fascinating young painter and writer, set out a few years ago to write a book about Crad, whom she had befriended. She had become one of Crad's few close friends. Lorette asked me if I thought Crad was an important writer. I'm not sure what an "important" writer is, unless we're talking the stature of Samuel Beckett or Virginia Woolf or John Ashbery. Crad has written some truly excellent stories. He cares about his words and his sentences: he is a perfectionist in that way. And within that framework, I think his writing is mostly about the content, the story, the jokes, the tragedy, and not about the writing itself. I mean, he isn't a great prose stylist, or an eccentric one in any way. Though he does have flashes of prose brilliance. (More on that later.) His eccentricity exists almost entirely in the content of his pieces. That said, he did play with form sometimes, and created some very fucked-up stories in that way. Although he can be extremely funny, I think many of his best pieces were the most serious ones, such as "One Rainy Night" (I hope I have the title right), about a guy helping his buddy move jars of shit (I hope I have the plot right). It was absurd but also heartbreaking.

Crad was important to me, as a model of DIY, and as a friend.

But then there's the issue of what I perceive as misogyny and racism in Crad's work. There may have been hints of it early on, but I think it became much more prominent later. I always felt that Crad's bitterness and misanthropy grew every year he stood on the street and watched all the morons walk by him, ignoring him. I certainly got pretty exasperated and angry out there at times, watching thousands of people walk by without noticing me standing there with a "Writer Going to Hell" sign around my neck.

I recently read a biography of E. E. Cummings and discovered that he'd been something of an anti-Semite (which Crad has never been); it shocked me, because Cummings was a pretty big hero to me as a kid. But in Cummings' journals, it seems it was "kike" this, and "jewboy" that, at least in the '40s and into the '50s. Pretty disappointing that such an intelligent man could have also embraced that particular ignorance and hatred. I haven't read through Crad's work in a long time. It's possible that those elements were always there, and it was me who changed, or grew to recognize those things in his writing.

As I wrote above, I learned recently that Crad is very sick. He's had more than one bout with cancer, and this time he isn't going to make it.

He and I haven't actually spoken in over a decade. Probably more like 15 years, though we've exchanged one or two brief emails.

The first public hint that things were going poorly in Kilodneyland was a remarkable story he posted on his blog. It's called "Dreaming with Jay." It's startling in its sincerity, its humanity.

It is Lorette who has made Crad's condition public, with his permission. I'm glad he has such a good friend in Lorette, and I hope he has a few others, too. But she says he is at peace with his situation.

April 2, 2014: I wrote what came above a few months ago. Today Lorette has reported that Crad is in his last days, or maybe his last hours. She says he is ready to go. He is at peace. My friend Steve Venright exchanged letters with Crad in the past month, and he too reports that Crad is at peace, and even spiritual — something I would never have imagined of Crad.

Lorette has written a great little book about Crad: *Kilodney Does Shakespeare, and Other Stories*. Academia has ignored him, but a fellow independista hasn't. Her book is a sort of ode to a hero — it's worshipful; but it's a great portrait of Crad post-street-selling, a Crad that most of us know little about. Crad co-operated in the book's writing, and offers a lot of his thoughts to Lorette.

The past while, I've been reading and re-reading Crad's 1990 story collection *Girl on the Subway* (Black Moss Press). The premise of this book is that it contains Crad's "serious" stories. (Though it precedes Crad's two major works of serious writing, *Excrement* and *Putrid Scum*, both from his own Charnel House imprint.) Even his serious stories contain more than a little of the absurd. But it's a beautiful book, and often heartbreaking. What really strikes me is what Crad so often does with the last paragraph of his stories: somehow all of his strengths as a prose writer become focused there. It's where you'll find the sublime.

Here's the close of "The Funeral of Lenny Zeller": "As I boarded the plane, I saw a girl who looked a lot like Cassandra Reyolds, and I thought it would be nice if we ended up sitting next to one another, but we didn't. I had a middle seat, and the window seat to my left was unoccupied. The sun had set by the time we took off, and the clouds were thick and violet as the plane climbed through them. I looked out the window, just letting my mind wander, and felt a twinge of sadness and loneliness for no particular reason. The reading light above me was on, and I reached up and switched it off. Then I rested my left hand upon the vacant seat and pretended to hold hands with Cassandra Reynolds's ghost."

And this is the last paragraph of "Henry": "Despite his medication, Henry does not fall asleep until very late at night. And every Tuesday and Friday morning around 7:30, when the garbage men come by, he hears them in his sleep, and he dreams that they are the angels come to pick him up."

I wish I had written Crad, and tried to make some connection again. Lorette says he's "feeling" the classical music she is playing for him. That was a few hours ago. Is he still alive now?

Here are the final two paragraphs of "A Moment of Silence for Man Ray": "The headlights of cars bumper to bumper on the boulevard were the funeral procession for another day thrown onto the trash heap of history. It was not surreal. It was as real as the hunger and the habit that anchored us to our work. / I had wasted several weeks doing nothing, but I did not waste that evening. I had to record what had otherwise died with me. I sat at the unpainted desk that faced the basement wall and gave a moment of silence to Man Ray. And as long as I was alive, one to myself too."

Good night, Crad.

April 2014

143

GOODBYE, CRUEL REPUTATION

IN A RECENT interview with Gary Barwin in the online mag *Jacket 2*, I said: "I am entering my literary decline (from not such a great height) reputation-wise, and I have neither the burden of fame nor agents nor audience expectation. There's a freedom in that. Besides, I don't want a complacent audience, however tiny that audience. With each book, or each writing project, I try to do something I've never done before, to push myself into a new discomfort zone. When I was in my 20s, I dreamed of writing a psychological suspense novel à la Patricia Highsmith. I know now that that will never happen, and that's freeing, too."

Gary asked me if I wanted to remove that first sentence — the one about being in my literary decline. He thought, perhaps, I was being hard on myself, as I often am. But in this case I wasn't. It was an expression of a) acceptance and b) celebration.

When I was younger, I thought that someday I might be a pretty well-known Canadian poet. But I've known for a long time now that that isn't going to be. I'm no Babstock, Solie, Hall, Connolly, Robertson, O'Meara, Dodds, or Queyras. What I am is a poetic weirdo. And that's a title I can heft up on my hunched shoulders and carry around with pride.

With my distance from Toronto, the city I left five years ago, after nearly half a century, I can actually feel myself becoming forgotten. There's a tiny *pop* every time I disappear from yet another person's consciousness. I'm like the Incredible Shrinking Man, wielding a giant safety pin to do battle with spiders. But it's not just the distance from Toronto that's precipitated my decline: it's that poetry has undergone a lot of changes, and what I write is not what wins the prizes or gets the residencies and other opportunities. It's a liberating experience. Very few people have any expectations of me. So I can do pretty much whatever I want.

Right now I'm finishing off a new poetry collection that is scheduled for release about the same time as this book. I decided I wanted that book to be different from anything I've ever published before. I want it to be my most reader-unfriendly poetry book. With my previous collections, I've been praised by reader friends mostly for the more narrative and transparently autobiographical poems I've written. I know many people would love a whole book of Razovsky poems — the character I created to reclaim my family's name, the name my paternal ancestors had before my dad and my grandfather Anglicized it to Ross. Everyone who's read them knows those poems are visceral and real and about *me*.

But I don't think there's ever going to be such a book. Instead, there's going to be *A Hamburger in a Gallery*, a crazed medley of weird shit, most of which I wrote in my own workshops. And all of my workshops are about trying new and crazy things. Some of the poems I've written in my Poetry Boot Camp or my Walking The Poem sessions have appeared in previous books, but they've mostly been balanced by more "normal" work. There will be no normal in this collection.

And the poetry collection I'm working on for a 2016 release will also be a book unlike any I've done before. It's going to be my attempt at a mainstream poetry book. If there can be such a thing as a mainstream poetry book. After that, I have no idea what will come. My book-length collaboration with Jaime Forsythe is about halfway done. Another few years and it'll be ready. It's fucking nuts. But I feel graced to alternate lines with Jaime, whose own poems are quirky genius I wish I'd written.

And then there's my fiction. I feel sort of sheepish, but I actually thought my 2012 novel *Snowball, Dragonfly, Jew* might become a modest hit and put my name on the map, any map — even some crumpled map gathering mould in the glove compartment of a rusting 1972 blue Valiant station wagon. I think it's a really good book. And it did get some very favourable reviews. And it won a small and lovely prize from a Jewish literary organization in Montreal. But it didn't make me slightly rich or even slightly famous. Right now, I'm working on a sequel to *SDJ*, but also working on a couple of other novels that will be completely nutso. I want to have written the Canadian *Joko's Anniversary*. Or the Canadian *Olt*. (You can look those up.)

I don't care about consistency or having a recognizable "voice" or winning anything anymore. I'm going to write as fast as I can, and do whatever I want, and hope that there are publishers who continue to support what I do. I've been lucky that way, at least. So far.

January 2015

ACKNOWLEDGEMENTS

Many thanks to my pal and partner-in-small-press-crime Nicholas Power for valuable feedback on "In the Small-Press Village: New Trends in Adequate Stapling" and for being such a consistent comrade in the racket. I'm grateful to Coach House Books editor and dear friend Alana Wilcox for commissioning the original version. Thanks, too, to Laurie Siblock, patient, supportive, sublime, who read the first drafts of most of these pieces and made excellent suggestions. I'm still pissed off with Brian Kaufman, but he did due diligence in wresting this book out of me, and I'm grateful for that. Thanks, too, to Karen Green, Shazia Hafiz Ramji, and everyone else at Anvil.

I continue to be inspired and amazed by both the persistent old-timers and the enthusiastic upstarts of the Canadian small-press publishing world. Thanks, Noelle Allen, Cameron Anstee, Kelsey Attard, Nelson Ball, Kemeny Babineau, Gary Barwin, derek beaulieu, David Caron, Michael e. Casteels, Victor Coleman, Linda Crosfield, jwcurry, Beverley Daurio, Jack David, Denis De Klerck, Paul Dutton, Amanda Earl, Greg Evason, Jon Paul Fiorentino, Beth Follett, Keith Henderson, Tim Inkster, Karl Jirgens, Brian Kaufman, Emily Keeler, Brian Lam, Kitty Lewis, rob mclennan, Christine McNair, Jay and Hazel MillAr, Leigh Nash, Hoa Nguyen, Mike O'Connor, Pearl Pirie, Nicholas Power, Meredith and Peter Quartermain, Sina Queyras, Karen Schindler, Rose and David Scollard, Dale Smith, Andrew Steeves, the late Richard Truhlar, Dan Wells, Silas White, Alana Wilcox, Carleton Wilson. And so many more.

INDEX

ABOUT THE AUTHOR

STUART ROSS has been involved in literary publishing for over 35 years. He is the author of nine books of poetry, two story collections, a previous book of personal essays, two collaborative novels, and a solo novel. He won the 2010 ReLit Prize for Short Fiction for *Buying Cigarettes for the Dog* and in 2012 was co-winner of the Mona Elaine Adilman Award for Fiction on a Jewish Theme for his novel *Snowball, Dragonfly, Jew.* In 2013 he was awarded the sole prize to an anglophone writer by l'Académie de la vie littéraire au tournant du 21e siècle for his poetry collection *You Exist. Details Follow.* Stuart lives in Cobourg, Ontario, and blogs at bloggamooga.blogspot.com.